What wi... ?

what do really want to know...

Answers to 101 Questions Teens Always Ask

MICHAEL FRANCIS PENNOCK

AVE MARIA PRESS
NOTRE DAME, INDIANA 46556

ate
can
ve?

ng

i?
hen they
church?

d about
t my
gain?

ho my
d you
ship?

What makes the Bible so special?
Where did it come from?
Was there a "real" Adam and Eve?
Do miracles happen today?
Did Jesus know he was God?
How can Jesus be both God and human?

Nihil Obstat: The Reverend Peter M. Mihalic, S.T.D., M. Div., Censor Deputas

Imprimatur: The Most Reverend Anthony M. Pilla, D.D., M.A., Bishop of Cleveland

Given at Cleveland, OH on 31 July 1995.

The *Nihil Obstat* and *Imprimatur* are official declarations that a book or pamphlet is free of doctrinal or moral error. No implication is contained therein that those who have granted the *Nihl Obstat* and *Imprimatur* agree with the contents, opinions, or statements expressed.

$\mathscr{D}$edication

$\mathscr{I}$ dedicate this book to the memory of Ronald Bugala. This outstanding Catholic gentleman was an exemplary husband, father, friend, and seeker of the Lord. All who knew Ron grew closer to the Lord because of him. He leaves as his legacy his loving wife, Carol, and four beautiful children.

Acknowledgments

I wish to thank my editor, Mike Amodei, for his invaluable help on this project. His gentle manner is a great source of encouragement to me.

I also wish to thank the various correspondents around the country who suggested questions for inclusion in this book.

Finally, I extend my gratitude to my loving daughter, Amy, and two outstanding students of mine, Kevin Amer and Steve Noga. They read my manuscript and reported to me that my answers made sense to them.

Ultimately, the Lord is the answer to our heart's longing and our deepest questions. May he bless those who read this book and grant them his joy and peace.

Contents

I broke my curfew and lied about where I was. How can I get my parents to trust me again?

I hate when people criticize me. Is there anything I can do about it?

Sometimes I'm not sure who my real friends are. How would you define true friendship?

What's wrong with hanging out with a certain group of people, like a clique?

How can I avoid peer pressure?

Lately, my friend talks about suicide. I'm not sure if she's putting me on. What should or can I do?

I've always had trouble understanding how Jesus is actually in the bread and wine? How is this so?

Why can't non-Catholics receive holy communion at Mass?

I can easily worship God on my own. Why do I need the church?

What is excommunication? For what reasons does a Catholic get excommunicated?

How do I know if I am doing right?

Is Natural Family Planning really an effective way to plan pregnancies?

How can Jesus be both God and human?

What is reincarnation? What does the church teach about reincarnation?

Introduction

*A*t the beginning of a term, I invite my students to write on index cards any questions they would like the course to address. Needless to say, after twenty-eight years of teaching nearly eight thousand teenagers, I have heard and collected hundreds of probing questions about life, faith, and the church. I've learned first-hand the truth of the saying "If you really want to learn, be a teacher." Throughout any given term, I try to devote part of one period per week to the questions from the index cards. I offer a brief response of my own and also open the floor to discussion. These sessions are some of the best of the entire course.

Most of the questions in *What We **Really** Want to Know* are taken directly from my collection of student index cards. Others have been submitted by teens, teachers, and youth ministers from around the country. Included are perennial, tough faith questions (for example, "Why does God allow innocent people to suffer?" and "Why do we have to die?"). My students have asked me these questions not as a mere academic exercise but because these issues touch their lives. They want to hear the how and why of the church's answers.

*What We **Really** Want to Know* addresses 101 questions in the areas of teen relationships, core Catholic teachings and practices, mysteries of life, sexuality, Christian living, and more. This book can be used as a springboard for discussions with teens.

In Catholic high schools, I recommend that teachers set aside about twenty minutes per week to read several of the questions and their respective answers, adding their own insights and opening the floor to student discussion and query.

Youth ministers can use the questions as a part of regular faith-sharing gatherings or even as a stimulus for a day or weekend retreat.

Parents can use the questions to help them answer similar ones posed by their own teenage son or daughter and to help begin a dialogue on these and other important issues.

Finally, *What We **Really** Want to Know* offers excellent supplementary reading for all Catholic teens who have important questions to be answered. While there are many books that address faith questions of adults, there are too few for teenagers. Teen questions deserve an attempt like this to answer them!

No matter how you personally choose to use this book, my hope for you is that you will continue to seek all answers in the Lord Jesus. God bless.

My parents put down all of my friends. Why do they do this?

I find it impossible to communicate with my parents. How can I improve?

How far do I have to go in obeying my parents?

Why should I honor my parents in religious matters when t

My par
They sa
immora

I broke
How ca

My dad
there a

Is it wr
the wis

I feel l
am?

I hate
can do

Sometimes I'm not sure who my real friends are. How would you define true friendship?

How can I make friends?

Is it wrong to break the confidence of a friend?

What's wrong with hanging out with a certain group of people, like a clique?

Chapter

1

Turn Up the Volume!

*Relationships with Parents
and Friends*

A psychologist was a well-known expert on parenting. He gave a lecture called "Ten Commandments for Parents." Then, he fell in love, married, and became a father and changed the title of the lecture to "Ten Hints for Parents." Another child arrived, and he began speaking on "Some Suggestions for Parents."

When the third child arrived, he stopped lecturing.

Parents quickly learn that children complicate any child-raising theory. You help your parents grow in wisdom and appreciation of the difficult task of growing up as they raise you in a complex, mostly anti-family society. Please be patient with them.

Patience is a good virtue for all relationships, including those with peers. Who hasn't had occasion to boil in anger when someone has stood you up or talked behind your back?

This chapter treats some questions today's teens have for relating to their parents, and others for relating to peers. Take some time to apply some of the questions and answers to your own life.

1

My parents put down all of my friends. Why do they do this?

Good parents always want the best for their children. From experience, they know that peer pressure is very difficult to resist and that your friends will have a powerful influence on you. Like many parents, they probably worry too much.

But ask yourself if your parents' concerns might be real. Consider these questions:

1. Are my friends a negative influence? Bad habits are easy to catch. Do my friends drink, drive recklessly, shoplift, cheat at school? If so, what effect do their examples have on me?

2. Am I a more honest person because of my friends or do I lie and cover up my whereabouts and my activities? Good friends will make you a better person. Bad friends will drag you down to their level.

3. Perhaps your mom and dad simply don't know your friends. If they did, maybe they'd like them. Are your friends respectful and considerate of your parents, or do they ignore your folks when they come over? Sometimes your parents may merely want your friends to acknowledge and talk to them. Make some time for you and your friends to visit with your folks instead of always being on the run. If this seems

uncomfortable for you to do, you might ask yourself what you are trying to hide.

4. Do your friends make pests of themselves, especially by calling on the phone at all hours and acting disrespectful when they ask for you? Most parents find non-stop phone calls or being treated rudely on the phone enough to drive them crazy.

Do you think your parents' standards too high? Do they treat all your friends—especially those of the opposite sex—as if they are not good enough for you? Be grateful you have parents who care, who love you, and who worry about the type of friends you associate with. Please take the time to communicate to your parents about your friends. Because they love you, they'll listen to your reasons for liking your particular friends. If you love your parents, you'll hear their concerns and work out some kind of compromise.

&

We ought to flee the friendship of the wicked.

~Epictetus, Greek philosopher

2
—

I find it impossible to communicate with my parents. How can I improve?

Communication is a tough art with anyone, let alone with parents who have authority over you. Undoubtedly, the age difference—also known as the "generation gap"—adds to problems in communication. You think you are right (and you may be). Parents think they are right (and they may be).

First, some general points. *Do* make an effort to communicate. Don't fall back on tired excuses for not communicating. For example:

"They don't take me seriously."
"We'll argue."
"They've already made up their minds."

Believe one of these and you won't even try to talk to your parents.

Second, play fair. Don't take on any roles or moods that block honest communication. Do you recognize yourself in any of the following descriptions?

Non-talker. You clam up and don't let them know your true thoughts and feelings.

Sulker. You let your anger seethe under the surface. Moping around the house is your way to get even.

Shouter. You think the loudest opinions are the right ones.

Sneaker. You let your parents think you will follow their directions, but then you do what you want anyhow.

Comparer. You play favorites with your parents by comparing them to one another or you belittle them by comparing them to your friends' folks who are "always better."

These mind games and many like them destroy dialogue between teens and their parents. And effective communication is a two-way exchange that involves both *speaking* and *listening.* Try the following strategy the next time you want to talk over an important issue with your mom or dad.

When you speak . . .

1. *Always be honest.*   Don't tell your folks what you think they want to hear simply to end the conversation.

2. *Don't blame.* Suspend judgment. Instead of saying, "You don't care" or "You don't have a clue," say "I'm not sure where you're coming from. Help me to understand."

3. *Seek mutual understanding.*   You are not in a war where there must be "winners" and "losers." The purpose of your conversation is to come to a peaceful resolution. Also, stick to one topic. Dragging out past hurts won't help to solve the current issue.

4. *Keep the noise level down.*   Loud arguing sheds more heat than light. Civilized conversation requires calm exchanges.

When you listen . . .

1. *Give your full attention.*   Hear the meanings of the words your parents are using. What are they feeling? Make eye contact. Notice non-verbal communication. All of these will help you pick up "unspoken messages" that are often at the heart of disagreements.

2. *Give them a chance to respond.*   Try not to anticipate what they are going to say. Be patient and hear them out. Don't interrupt.

3. *Empathize.* Put yourself in their shoes. What would *you* say if you were the parent? Above all, realize they love you and are trying to do their best.

4. *Remember.* Don't forget what they've told you the minute after they've said it. In fact, repeat what they said to let them know you've understood them.

The most important rule for both speaking and listening is love. It's hard to get angry when you know the dialogue begins and ends in love. Love thrives on communication. The effort is worth it. Don't give up. Ask Jesus to bless you and your parents as you engage in dialogue. He'll be with you to help you all grow into a closer family. Be sure to ask for his help.

When I was fourteen years old, I thought my father was an old ignoramus. When I became twenty-one, I was surprised at how much the old man had learned in seven years.

~Mark Twain

Thorny Issues

Practice the steps for effective speaking and listening with your parents using one or more of the following "thorny issues" as a starting point. Take note of which steps worked well, ways to improve, and the results of your conversation.

- Establishing a good curfew time and a fair punishment if you violate a curfew.

- Drinking before the age of twenty-one.

- Whether or not parents have the right to look through their teen's belongings.

- What determines positive music.

3

How far do I have to go in obeying my parents?

There was once a little boy playing in the garden of his father's mission outpost in the Belgian Congo. Suddenly, his father yelled at him: "Philip, obey me instantly—get down on your belly." The boy listened at once as his father continued, "Now crawl to me fast." The boy obeyed. When he was 15 yards closer, the father instructed, "Now stand and run to me." The boy ran into his father's arms. When he looked back, he saw a fifteen-foot boa constrictor hanging from a tree's branch directly over the place where he was playing.[1]

Parents love this story because the boy gave his father instant obedience. There were no complaints or excuses like: "Tell me why," "In a little while," or "Do I hafta?"

The fourth commandment obliges you to obey your parents. Both the books of Exodus and Deuteronomy use the word *honor* to encompass the virtue of *obedience* when they record this commandment. The New Testament shows the link between these two words:

Children, be obedient to your parents in the Lord—that is what uprightness demands. The first commandment that has a promise attached to it is: *Honor your father and your mother,* and the promise is: *so that you may have long life and prosper in the land* (Eph 6:1-3).

Note that God rewards those who honor their parents. God has willed that parents have authority over their children and that children should obey them.

What if your folks make unreasonable demands? As a teen, you do have the right to express your views. You can make an effort to change their minds. Badgering and sulking, however, are counterproductive and signs of immaturity. And, if your parents still insist on a particular course of action, you must obey.

Parents, like everyone else, are imperfect and do sometimes err in their judgments. Also, they sometimes act on "hunches," thus they cannot always explain their reasons for requiring something of you. You still owe them honor, respect, and obedience. A good rule of thumb: As long as you live in your parents' house, you should obey their rules and commands. It is a sin to disobey.

The one exception to obeying your parents is if they order you to do something you know is immoral. Obedience to God's law overrides the responsibility to obey one's parents.

The ancient philosopher Aristotle insightfully wrote, "Wicked men obey from fear, good men, from love." Obeying your parents is an act of love.

4
—

Why should I honor my parents in religious matters when they don't even go to church?

A father was complaining about his family's television viewing habits:

> The kids are always watching sitcoms and neglecting their homework. The wife has an addiction to the soaps and late-afternoon talk shows. My dinner is always late. As soon as the football season is over, I'm going to pull the plug.

This story illustrates the nature of hypocrisy, the "do-as-I-say-not-as-I-do" approach to life. In one way or another, everyone is a hypocrite. We aspire to and profess high ideals and values. But we often fall short of achieving them. This inability to follow through is part of the human condition, our fallen nature that needs Christ's redemption. St. Paul, a determined and faith-filled Christian who even died for his beliefs, knew this human frailty well when he wrote:

> $\mathcal{I}$do not understand my own behavior; I do not act as I mean to, but I do things that I hate. . . . The good thing I want to do, I never do; the evil thing which I do not want—that is what I do (Rm 7:15,19).

It is wrong for parents and other adults to preach one standard to you and yet fail to put it into practice themselves. They need to change. They need gentle reminding that actions speak louder than words. They need to reflect on their parental and adult responsibility to give good example.

A sign of maturity on your part is to accept and love less-than-perfect people, especially your parents. Just because they fail to follow through does not mean that your religious practices are not worthwhile. The practice of faith is both true and good. Please continue to do the right thing even if your parents don't. In the meantime, consider doing the following:

1. Let *your* actions speak loudly and clearly. Your good example may influence your parents to once again do what they know is right.

2. Pray for your parents. They need to hear the Holy Spirit call them to their responsibilities.

3. Gently bring up this topic in conversation with your folks. Talk calmly and without judgment. Your delicate questioning may speak to their hearts.

4. Talk this over with adults you respect; perhaps a parish priest, a teacher, or a grandparent. Their insights and encouragement will help you deal with the ambiguity you have discovered. They may also offer further strategies for working through this situation.

5
—

My parents give me grief over the music I listen to. They say that it is immoral. Can music be immoral?

Music is one of God's great gifts to us. Good music inspires, soothes, lightens our hearts, energizes, celebrates, evokes deep feelings, and lifts us to the heavens. Herbert Spencer wrote, "Music must rank as the highest of the fine arts—as the one which, more than any other, ministers to human welfare."

Music, like any good gift from God, can be perverted and misused. For example, misuse of wine leads to alcoholism. Or a perversion of sex causes deviant, harmful, and debasing behavior. How do you judge if the music you listen to is good or bad? Jesus gave effective guidelines to follow when he told us to judge things by their fruits (Mt 7:16-18). In other words, if something is good, it will bear good fruit. Ask yourself if your music enhances any of the "fruits of the Holy Spirit." Does your music make you more:

- 🎵 loving?
- 🎵 peaceful?
- 🎵 kind?
- 🎵 faithful?
- 🎵 joyful?
- 🎵 patient?
- 🎵 generous?
- 🎵 mild?
- 🎵 chaste?

If so—and a lot of contemporary Christian music does—it is probably good.

On the other hand, music is wrong or immoral when it produces bad fruit. Be wary of lovely rhythms and seductive beats; sometimes there is no connection between the rhythms and beats of the music and a song's lyrics. Also ask yourself if the music you listen to:

✗ enflames your anger?

✗ encourages promiscuous sex?

✗ promotes self-pity?

✗ endorses escapism through drugs or alcohol?

✗ glamorizes a life of selfish materialism?

✗ approves of Satanism?

You might also examine the lifestyles of your favorite musicians. Do these "stars" deserve your support? Are they respectable and loving people, the kind of people you would be happy to hold up to a young child as a role model? Do they call forth the best in *you*?

Avoid music and performers (as well as movies, magazines, and television programs) that produce bad fruit. Remember the warning of computer programmers: "Garbage in, garbage out."

Rock Line

Think over and/or discuss the following questions:

- Who are your favorite musicians? Are they good role models?

- Agree or disagree. Christians should boycott performers whose lifestyles promote sex, drugs, materialism, violence, or selfishness.

- Analyze the lyrics of at least two of your current favorite songs for the values they promote.

6

I broke my curfew and lied about where I was. How can I get my parents to trust me again?

Trust is hard to win back once lost. Consider the example of the bank clerk who was about to get a promotion and a hefty raise from the bank president. But in the cafeteria line one day, the bank president saw the clerk hide two extra pats of butter under his bread, worth a total of five cents. Then and there, the bank president decided against the raise and promotion. He reasoned that if the clerk cheated in small things, he could not trust him at all.

By lying to your folks, you probably have made them suspicious about the hours you keep, how you use the car and spend your money, the integrity of the people you date, whether you drink or not, and whether you tell them the truth all the time. Though regaining your parents' trust may be difficult, it is not impossible. Here are three good habits that can help:

1. *Apologize and mean it.* Everyone deserves a second chance. Your parents realize this. It is difficult for a loving parent not to forgive a genuinely sorry teen who slips up occasionally.

2. *Communicate openly.* From this time forward, don't pull any surprises. Let your parents know your plans and any changes that develop. Minutes seem like hours to a worried parent. For example, if you're going to be late, always call. Your mom or dad want to know you're OK.

3. *Be truthful.* Don't shade the truth or cut corners. Remember the bank clerk. It is attention to the little things that creates a treasury of trust. If you want your mom and dad to trust you again, you must be honest, a person of your word. Follow through on what you say. With time and patient follow-through on your part, your parents will begin to believe and trust you again.

7

My dad's drinking is tearing our family apart. Is there anything I can do?

Alcoholism is a physical and psychological addiction to alcohol. It is a disease that develops in stages. An alcoholic may be a person who needs a drink every day, uses alcohol to reduce tension, or can't stop drinking once he or she starts.

Unfortunately, alcoholics don't often recognize their problem, or they vigorously deny it. Their denial leads to promises they don't keep and prevents them from getting help on their own.

Knowing these basic facts can help you understand your dad's behavior. And there are things you can do. Tell your dad you love him, are concerned about his behavior, and are willing to help. Include your mom and other family members in on the conversation as well. Your next steps should involve:

> *working with an alcoholism counselor.* Act now by finding a good alcoholism counselor. Your pastor or diocesan Catholic Charities office can usually recommend a trained professional. The counselor will likely recommend some form of *intervention,* a technique in which the alcoholic is confronted with the truth about his or her behavior and its effect on others. The goal of intervention is to get medical help for the abuser and psychological support to help him or her stay sober in the future.

> *contacting your local Alateen and Al-Anon groups.* Alateen is a support group for teenagers whose parents are alcoholics. Al-anon is a group that helps spouses of alcoholics. These groups can help you learn how to help your dad and also help yourself with the difficult challenge of living with an alcoholic.

> *praying for your dad.* He is sick. The Lord came to help sick people. Ask for his healing love to touch your family.

loving your dad. His self-esteem is low. He'll need your support and encouraging words as he begins his recovery.

God bless you as you face this family problem. And remember, now is the time to act. Please seek help. You can help to save your father's life.

For Reference

Check the phone book for the following numbers:

Alcoholics Anonymous:

Alateen:

Al-Anon:

8
—

Is it wrong for me to see an R-rated movie against the wishes of my parents?

You definitely owe your parents your respect and obedience (see Question 3). In regards to R-rated movies, your parents are wise in denying you permission to see them. They want you to have a healthy body, as well as a healthy mind and spirit. Films with an R-rating are objectionable on at least one of these counts: vulgar and obscene language, violence, or explicit sex scenes.

Foul language is almost a norm in today's society; its use represents a decline in civility. One popular film used the "f"-word 294 times (said on the average of twice per minute). It tried to lend "realism" to its characters. Many of today's films are violent and underscore the violence in our nation. As social scientists increasingly agree, there is a connection between TV and movie violence and the cheapening of human life.

Explicit sex scenes underscore promiscuity or adultery. They attack the sanctity of committed sexual love that only marriage can support. Perhaps more dangerous than the sex scenes themselves—which can enflame lust—is the unquestioning promotion of immoral sexual practices that undermine family life and Christian values. One has to question the imagination of filmmakers who offend rather than ennoble their audiences.

If you feel strongly about seeing a particular R-rated film because of its historic, artistic, or educational value, ask your parents to see it with you. Then discuss it with them. Viewing an R-rated film is not the worst you can do as a teen. But swallowing its message without thinking is dangerous. You should be a critical judge not only of today's movies, but also of other forms of media like music, advertisements, books, magazine articles, and electronic forums. Be part of the debate in today's cultural war for people's minds.

9

I feel like a failure. Why is everyone better than I am?

In reality, no one is better than anyone else. God loves us all equally and unconditionally. As the poster says, *God doesn't make junk.* We are different, unique sons and daughters of God. Just because your little finger is not the same as your ring finger is not to say that the ring finger is better. It is different, that's all. So it is with you and those you are comparing yourself to.

Many teens suffer from a negative self-image, often described as an "inferiority complex," which leads them to think everyone is better than they are. This unhealthy attitude results in a pessimistic outlook and overdue concern about one's appearance or performance. It also can lead to a lack of self-confidence, shyness, bitterness, and a host of other social problems.

Comparing yourself with others is usually nonproductive because you will always discover someone who is smarter, better-looking, more socially adept, more physically fit, and so forth, than you are. Comparisons can also lead to pride and an inflated ego, especially if you are more skilled in one or more areas than someone you know. However, in reality, you are neither inferior nor superior to others as a *person*. Here are some tips for improving your self-image:

★ *Remember to look at yourself from God's point of view.* God created you specially from among countless other possibilities. Jesus died on the cross looking into your eyes and pouring out his love on you.

★ *Stop comparing yourself to others.* Rather, look to Jesus as the measure of what it means to be a "together" person. Read the gospels to find out more about the things Jesus valued. He said we can discover our true selves when we love and serve others.

★ *Try something new.* Stretch your mind, your body, your emotions, your spirit. Master a new skill. By developing and discovering your gifts, you will enhance your self-image.

★ *Laugh at yourself . . . often.* You are not perfect. You'll make mistakes; everyone does. Learn from them and move on.

★ *Look at the bright side of things.* Appreciate the joy of simply being alive. Take in the splendor of nature. Savor good food. Delight in the exciting competition of a sporting event. Enjoy observing the innocence of a baby. Remember, negative thoughts about yourself or others make for a miserable existence. A joyful attitude which looks at everything as a gift from God, including yourself, leads to a fulfilling life.

The Optimist and the Pessimist

Some parents were at their wits' end over their twin boys—one an eternal optimist, the other a hopeless pessimist. Finally, they went to a psychiatrist who devised what he thought would be a sure-fire remedy.

The doctor placed the optimist in a room filled with manure and told him to dig, figuring this would cure him of his joyful nature. He put the pessimist in a room filled with toys and told him to play. This was bound to cheer the sad-faced boy.

But when the doctor returned with the parents some hours later, he was flabbergasted at the results. The little pessimist was bawling, complaining that he would hurt himself if he played with the toys. The little optimist, on the other hand, was furiously digging in the manure. When his mother asked what he was doing, the boy joyfully exclaimed, "With all this manure, there must be a pony around somewhere!"

10

I hate when people criticize me. Is there anything I can do about it?

Abraham Lincoln said this about the many criticisms leveled against him:

> If I were to try to read, much less answer, all the attacks made on me, this shop might as well be closed for any other business. I do the very best I know how—the very best I can; and I mean to keep doing so until the end. If the end brings me out all right, what is said against me won't amount to anything. If the end brings me out wrong, ten angels swearing I was right would make no difference.

It takes a strong person to handle disapproval so generously. Lincoln's point is this: *Try your best and persist, despite the criticism.*

In addition, be yourself. Don't be fake simply to avoid someone's negativity. Remember the famous advice from Shakespeare's *Hamlet* :

> *This above all: to thine own self be true;*
> *And it must follow, as the night the day,*
> *Thou canst not then be false to any man.*

Fortunately, most people will be gracious enough to accept you for who you are. But not everyone will, especially other teens who put tremendous pressure on their peers to conform, to follow the crowd.

Try your best to be true to yourself. But if people criticize you, investigate why. If they condemn you because they can't tolerate your effort or honesty, then *they* have a problem. *You are not at fault.* You have no obligation to live up to their expectations.

However, sometimes criticism is valid and can be helpful. For example, perhaps you are always late or unkempt or loud or lazy. These habits—and many others like them—are traits over which you do have some control. Listen to the reminders of people who care about you and accept them as helps, not hurts. With God's help and persistent effort on your part, you can change these negative behavior patterns.

Also, ask your friends to evaluate any criticism directed at you. They'll know if the criticism is worthwhile or merely sour grapes. Friends can help you cope with the pettiness of other people. Remember, too, to turn to Jesus, who loves you unconditionally and understands you perfectly. Finally, pray the famous *Serenity Prayer* to give you strength:

> *G*od, give me grace to accept with serenity
> the things that cannot be changed,
> courage to change the things which should be changed,
> and the wisdom to distinguish the one from the other.

11

Sometimes I'm not sure who my real friends are. How would you define true friendship?

The famous poet Lord Byron displayed the meaning of true friendship this way: One day at school he saw a senior beating on his friend unmercifully. Byron had a clubfoot and was in no position to defend his friend. Nevertheless, he approached the ruffian and asked him how many punches he intended to inflict on his bloodied friend. "Why do you care?" sarcastically responded the bully. "Because, if you please," replied the trembling Byron, "I will take half of them."

True friends suffer for each other. They are one. If one hurts, the other hurts. The ancient Greek philosopher Aristotle described friendship as "a single soul dwelling in two bodies." A Native American tribal expression for the word friend means "one-who-carries-my-sorrow-on-his-back."

It would be good to analyze how the people you consider to be friends stack up to these descriptions. For whom would you be willing to take blows? This is not always an easy question to answer because many people you call friends are something other than committed, true friends. True friends might be defined as those who know the real you—your secrets, dreams, hurts, and joys.

We sometimes refer to acquaintances as friends. However, an acquaintance is simply a person we know by name or face. Neighbors or classmates usually fit this category. Dedicated, close friends, on the other hand, exhibit the following characteristics:

☆ *Loyalty.* Friends stick up for each other. They are dependable.

☆ *Listening skills.* Friends really pay attention to what the other is saying and feeling.

☆ *Time.* Friends spend time together. And they can be together comfortably without talking. As someone said, "Pals I do something with. Friends I do nothing with."

☆ *Thoughtfulness.* Friends put themselves in each other's shoes. They know how to help out in times of need.

☆ *Encouragement.* Friends bring out the best in each other. They show care by cheering each other in bad, depressing times. They also challenge each other to try something new.

☆ *Honesty.* Friends lovingly tell the truth to each other. They also express their anger without being destructive.

☆ *Sense of humor.* Friends enjoy a good laugh together. And they can chuckle at their mistakes without ill will.

☆ *Confidence.* True friends keep secrets.

☆ *Acceptance.* Friends allow each other to be themselves. They give each other space in their relationship.

☆ *Authenticity.* Friends are down-to-earth, not transparent or phony. For example, they can talk openly about their affection for each other and not be embarrassed.

☆ *Forgiveness.* Friends have learned how to say, "I am sorry" and "I forgive you."

How many of these characteristics do you recognize in yourself? In someone you call friend?

12
—
How can I make friends?

Making friends can be exciting, scary, fun, and challenging all at once. Here are some ways you can make new friends:

1. *Be yourself.*   Accept the special person you are. Phony people attract phony friends.

2. *Be open.*   Accept others for who they are. Don't try to change them into your ideal. Be willing to make friends with people of different ages, genders, interests, cultures, and the like.

3. *Get involved.*   Friendships often arise when people have common interests. Play sports, join clubs at school, be part of a parish youth group. You're bound to find like-minded people who want to be your friends.

4. *Talk to people.*   Ask questions. Show interest in their responses. Be willing to share your thoughts and feelings if others want to know about you.

5. *Listen.*   Everyone finds a good listener attractive. Make eye contact. Don't interrupt when someone is talking. Show you are listening by occasionally rephrasing what someone said.

6. *Smile.*   People want to be with those who radiate happiness. A smile is an invitation to friendship.

7. *Be an interesting person.*   Cultivate many interests— sports, politics, music, movies, hobbies. A person who has only one interest is often very boring. Boring friends are not often in demand!

8. *Be persistent and patient.*   Friendships take time to develop. If at first you don't succeed, don't quit. If you work at the other rules, someone will eventually discover you and cherish being your friend. As Benjamin Franklin once advised: "Be slow in choosing a friend, slower in changing."

Above all, remember that you never lose in friendship unless you refuse the friendship of Jesus. He calls you his friend (see Jn 15:15). His love for you is unconditional and everlasting. Furthermore, he proved his love by dying for you.

If you let Jesus' love touch you, then you will naturally want to love God and others. "Let us love, then, because he first loved us" (1 Jn 4:19). By being a loving friend of Jesus, you will become very attractive to other people who desperately want the love of a true Christian.

The only way to have a friend is to be one.

~Ralph Waldo Emerson

Friendliness Quotient

Do you have the makings to attract friends? Are you easy to get to know? Rate your friendliness quotient according to this scale:

4 — always   **3** — usually   **2** — sometimes   **1** — never

_____ 1. I smile often and am usually in a good mood.

_____ 2. I feel comfortable in my peer group, even if I don't know everyone.

_____ 3. I make strangers (like a new classmate) feel welcome.

_____ 4. I'm at ease around adults.

_____ 5. I keep up with the news and can converse easily about it.

_____ 6. I have many interests and like talking about them.

_____ 7. I'm respectful of people of all ages.

_____ 8. I try to listen to people when they speak to me, even if they are boring.

_____ 9. I like to ask questions of people.

_____ 10. I have a good sense of humor and can even laugh at my own mistakes.

Add your scores. If you have 35 points or above, you likely make new friends easily and often. If you have 25-34 points, you have an above-average friendliness quotient. If you are below 24 points, you have room for improvement. Improving any of the above will enhance your chances of making friends.

13

——

Is it wrong to break the confidence of a friend?

In general, "keeping secrets" is a major element of friendship. Thus, breaking the confidence of a friend usually damages the loyalty and trust on which friendship thrives.

But there are exceptions, especially when you suspect your friend is being hurt, or is going to hurt himself or herself or someone else. For example, perhaps your friend tells you of being abused and refuses to tell anyone other than you. Or maybe your friend is dropping hints about suicide. In both cases, you should go to an adult for immediate help—for example, a parent, priest, counselor, family friend, or sensitive teacher.

Avoid the trap of "promising not to tell" if pressured to do so. Your word is your honor, so be careful before promising anything. Rather, tell your friend: "I cherish our friendship. I'd never talk if it's best not to do so. But I can't promise ahead of time if I don't know what your secret is.

Our friendship is strong enough that if you don't want me to know, I'll understand."

Imaginings

Suppose you could have as a friend any one man and any one woman alive today, no matter how famous. Who would they be? Why?

Suppose you had only a week to live. Which friends would you spend it with? Why? What would you do? Would you want to be alone any of the time? Why or why not?

14
—
What's wrong with hanging out with a certain group of people, like a clique?

A story helps us see why cliques present problems:

A religious Master was commenting that a major evil effect of religion is that it splits humanity into sects. To illustrate, he told of the little boy who asked the neighbor girl, "Are you Catholic?"

"No," she replied with self-importance. "We belong to another abomination!"

The girl meant, of course, denomination. But it is an abomination, something to detest, when we exclude others from our circle or feel superior to others for any reason.

By definition, a *clique* is "an exclusive group of friends or associates." You probably belong to groups where individuals have similar interests—for example, sports, music, drama—but your groups are not exclusive. You'll let any interested person join. This kind of group is OK and even very valuable as you grow and develop your social skills, interests, and gifts. We all need friends and companions who enjoy what we enjoy.

But when groups become exclusive, they can be destructive. True cliques exclude rather than include. The "jocks" might strut around and arrogantly look down on others. The "burnouts" might sit on the sidelines, making fun of others who don't drink or do drugs. The "beautiful people" might be so awe-struck over their wealth and good looks that they have no time for the ordinary folk. The "nerds" might bond together for self-defense against others who envy their brains. Every school has its cliques, though their names change from place to place and year to year. What remains constant is that most cliques do not contribute to school spirit or unity.

What Do You Say?

◆ Give names for five cliques at your school. Are they destructive or constructive? Explain.

◆ Can you be popular at your school and not be a member of a clique? Why or why not?

15

How can I avoid peer pressure?

First of all, not all peer pressure is bad and does not necessarily need to be avoided. Peer pressure is the group's influence on us to conform to its outlook on life, its values, and its way of behaving.

Peer pressure can be *positive* (like a group of classmates deciding to visit a sick classmate) or *neutral* (for example, having the same hair style or wearing the same baseball cap). *Negative* peer pressure is the problem. It is conformity that can turn people into sheep.

A recent television documentary showed how easily sheep can be led. Hundreds of sheep were confined in a large pen at a slaughterhouse. To get them to walk up a narrow ramp, the slaughterhouse owners trained a goat to lead them. The goat began its job by milling in their midst. It then began to walk up the ramp and, after advancing five feet, paused and looked at the sheep. Soon, one sheep then another nervously began to follow the goat. When the goat got to the top of the ramp, it passed through a gate on the left which was quickly closed. The sheep, however, proceeded through a gate on the right. One after another ambled to its death.

Negative peer pressure can destroy your individuality. It may even persuade you to go against your own morals. "Everyone is doing it," you may reason. It being smoking, cheating, drinking, shoplifting, driving wildly, engaging in sex, mocking an unpopular student, and the like. "Acceptance at any cost" can make you a superficial and phony person. As the sheep found out, going along with the crowd can also end in tragedy.

Resisting negative peer pressure is tough in today's world. But to develop into a healthy adult you have to learn to do it as a teenager. Here are seven things you can do to help you ward off negative peer pressure:

1. *Be clear about what you value.* How is what the crowd wants you to do different from what you stand for? Write down your deeply felt convictions. For example, "Because I respect my body, I will never do drugs." Frequently reread your list. Determine never to compromise your convictions.

2. *Resolve to be yourself always.* True friends won't make you do something you don't want to do. They will admire you for your courage and standing up for your beliefs.

3. *Say "no" gracefully but firmly.* If you are asked to justify your answer this is your clue that the person has not accepted it. Any reason you give is likely to be challenged. Repeat your "no." For example, simply say, "No, thanks. I don't drink and I want to keep it that way."

4. *Avoid tempting situations where others may pressure you to compromise your values.* There once was a king who interviewed some potential chariot drivers for the job of chauffeuring him around the kingdom. He asked each driver how close he could come to the edge of a high, winding mountain road. The first replied, "I'm so skilled, I could drive within a foot of the edge." The second boasted, "I could drive within six inches." But the third responded, "I would stay as far away from the edge as possible." The king chose the third driver, who cared more for the king's safety than his driving prowess.

   Christians likewise avoid risky situations that can lead to trouble. To honor their king—Jesus—they stay clear of tempting and dangerous situations.

5. *Examine your peer group.* If a particular group you hang around with is constantly pressuring you to do wrong, then maybe you should start looking for a new group to spend time with. Sometimes it's better (and easier) to do without certain people than trying to convince these so-called friends that some of their activities are simply not right.

6. *Join some organizations at school or in your parish.* You're bound to meet some good, like-minded people by getting involved.

7. *Pray.* Ask the Lord to send you some good friends who share your values. Ask the Holy Spirit to strengthen in you the gifts of fortitude and prudence. Jesus promised he would send good things to those who ask him. Why not take him up on the offer?

16

—

I get depressed at times and even think about suicide. Is this normal?

About one in four high-school students have had suicidal thoughts at one time or another. But only one in five of this group has actually have tried it, and only 2 percent of these actually injure themselves.

These statistics should convince you that you are not alone if you've thought of suicide. You might ask yourself *why* you are having these thoughts. The likely reason is depression.

But please don't think that occasionally being down in the dumps means that you are suicidal. It's natural to feel depressed when you're cut from a team, a boyfriend or girlfriend drops you for no apparent reason, you go to a new school and no one cares that you exist, your parents are breaking up, a grandmother dies. You should be concerned, however, when the depression lasts for weeks at a time and you're so absorbed in your problem that you have little energy for anything else.

Temporary, mild depression is normal. A good antidote to occasional depression is to get out and do things. Moping does not make the feeling go away. Wallowing in self-pity feeds on itself and can distort reality.

Another help is to talk over your feelings with a friend. Life has its ups and downs. It is very good for your psychological health to share your feelings with others. The sharing process might even help you determine the reason for your hurt. And your friends can reassure you of two important lessons: (1) You are worthwhile. (2) You have people you can depend on during tough times.

But if you are beyond just an occasional fleeting thought about suicide and are actually contemplating it, please gather enough strength to seek help. Don't keep your hurting a secret. There are many people who are willing to help you.

God loves you and has given you a unique, beautiful life to live. God also loves you through other people—teachers, priests, relatives, friends. Talk to them. They will help you look at your problems more objectively. They will reassure you of their great love for you. And when you know you are loved, you will want to embrace life and enjoy all the good times worth living for.

More Teenage Suicide Statistics

◆ Approximately 5,000 teens kill themselves each year.

◆ Between 400,000-800,000 teens attempt suicide each year.

◆ Suicide is the second leading cause of death among teens.

◆ Most teens know someone who has tried or completed suicide.

◆ Each suicide intimately affects at least six other people.

◆ More girls than boys attempt suicide, but boys "succeed" 80 percent more often.

◆ Most suicidal persons do not want to die.

17

—

Lately, my friend talks about suicide. I'm not sure if she's putting me on. What should or can I do?

Talking about suicide and death is itself a warning sign. You must be a good friend if she is willing to confide in you. Here's how you can help:

⇨ *Keep talking to her.* She needs someone to listen and not judge. Give your friend your respect and attention. Praise her good points whenever you can. Let her know how special she is and how you treasure your friendship. Be direct and open.

➪   *Pay attention to any of these suicide warning signs:*
    —**withdrawal from you or other friends**
    —**moodiness and anger**
    —**risk-taking**
    —**failing at school**
    —**a change in eating patterns (including no appetite)**
    —**loss of sleep**
    —**uncontrollable crying**
    —**heavy drinking or drug use**
    —**loss of interest in usual social activities**
    —**giving away prized possessions**

➪   *Don't promise you'll keep it secret.*   Her life is at stake. Tell her that you want to get help.

➪   *Involve an adult.*   Do not handle this situation alone. Ask the help of a priest, counselor, parent, or teacher.

➪   *If you think your friend is in immediate danger, don't leave her alone.*   Wait until there is no threat of danger before you go for help.

➪   *Pray.*   Ask God for wisdom and strength for both you and your friend.

Is your friend's sharing these suicidal thoughts simply an attention-getting device? It could be, but you don't know for sure. Most people who try suicide are not crazy and often appear quite normal. But they really feel helpless, hapless, and hopeless. They are not thinking clearly and so turn their negative thoughts inward. Counselors are very effective in helping most suicidal persons turn their negative self-image into positive self-esteem. Play it safe. *Take any threat of suicide seriously.*

You may also wonder how God views suicide. Suicide involves serious matter. If done with knowledge and consent, it is mortally sinful, a violation of the fifth commandment. But only God can judge the state of a person's soul. Certainly, many suicides result when seriously depressed, emotionally upset people distort reality. Their emotions might limit their freedom to grasp fully the serious impact of the evil they are doing. And limited freedom lessens blame worthiness.

One final point: Suicide is never glamorous. It offends a loving God and wastes God's beautiful gift of life. Suicide punishes the human community by depriving it of one of its precious members. And it scars the memories of those who loved the suicide victim. Friends and relatives will often feel guilty and ask, "Could I have done something to save a life?"

Pray for your friend and all those who conclude that life is not worth living.

For Reference

Check the phone book under "Suicide" or "Suicide Prevention." Record helpful numbers in the spaces below:

National Number 1-800-621-4000

What is the point of infant baptism? Shouldn't a person be old enough to be able to choose his or her faith?

I've always had trouble understanding how Jesus is actually in the bread and wine? How is this so?

Why can't non-Catholics receive holy communion at Mass?

I do
real

Wh
supp
supp

My
year
told
agai

Is a
it so

I ca
need

Som
same. On the other hand, my grandfather told me that the Catholic church is the only true church. Which is it?

Does God save non-Catholics? After all, the majority of people are not Catholic and may not even heard of Jesus or the church.

More and more it seems as if the media are blatantly anti-Catholic. Why do so many people hate Catholics and the Catholic church?

Chapter

2

You Mean I Have to Go to Mass EVERY Sunday?

Looking at Catholic Teachings About
Sacraments, Sins, and Salvation

A famous coach responded to the question of how much pro football contributes to physical fitness in America. "Very little," he replied. "At a pro game, fifty thousand spectators, desperately needing exercise, sit in the stands watching twenty-two men who desperately need rest."

Some would say it is like that with the church. Many are idle spectators on the sidelines while too few create all the action.

As you read the answers to the following questions on the church and the sacraments, you might ask yourself whether you aim to play or merely watch.

A second story helps to focus on another issue covered in this chapter: morality. It is the famous story about the famed American writer and naturalist, Henry David Thoreau. He chose to go to jail rather than to pay a poll tax to support the Mexican War, which he thought was immoral. Like others at the time, he concluded that the war was a move to enlarge slave-holding states. And he could and would not support slavery.

His friend, Ralph Waldo Emerson, also an abolitionist, visited Thoreau in jail and asked, "Henry, why are you here?"

Thoreau replied, "Waldo, why are you *not* here?"

To be a Christian means to act morally and accept the responsibilities of being God's children. And not merely standing on the sidelines.

18

—

What is the point of infant baptism? Shouldn't a person be old enough to be able to choose his or her faith?

Some Christian denominations, the Baptists, for example, accept the logic of this question by refusing to baptize infants. The Catholic church's long-standing tradition of infant baptism boils down to these key truths:

1. *Salvation is God's gift, not a human achievement.* Infant baptism underscores the belief in God's unconditional love, God's own initiative and election. No one deserves God's love. God's grace, providence, and choice bring people into the Christian family. When the church baptizes infants, it acknowledges that God is the dispenser of gifts, not humans.

2. *Infant baptism is a traditional practice.* The *Catechism of the Catholic Church* puts it this way:

   There is explicit testimony to this practice from the second century on, and it is quite possible that, from the beginning of the apostolic preaching, when whole "households" received baptism, infants may also have been baptized (CCC, 1252; see also Acts 16:15,33;18:8;1 Cor 1:16).

3. *Jesus welcomed all into the kingdom.* The baptism of children flows naturally from Jesus' own attitude to them. Jesus instructed his apostles to allow children to come to him (Mk 10:14-16) and taught all of his followers to approach God with childlike faith. Children are wonderful examples of the simple openness required for the gospel to take root and bear fruit in each of our lives.

4. *Parents inevitably will share their values with their children.* For example, a little boy was afraid of the dark, and one stormy night he called out to his mother. She said to him, "Everything is all right. God loves you and is watching over you." The little guy responded, "I know. But right now I need someone with skin on." Parents and the entire Christian community are Jesus in-the-flesh to children. Children meet Jesus in their parents and family members from the day of their birth. This experience will serve as the basis for their own growing acceptance of faith as they become adults.

5. *Baptism forgives original sin, adopts us into God's family, and makes us heirs to eternal life.* Baptism is the ordinary means of transmitting these graces God has entrusted to the Christian community (Jn 3:5). These graces, or benefits, extend to both adults and infants. Finally, the church takes seriously Jesus' command to baptize (Mt 28:19) and extends the fruits of this privilege to all.

19

—

I've always had trouble understanding how Jesus is actually in the bread and wine? How is this so?

This question deals with the "real presence" of Christ in the eucharist. Above all else, the eucharist is a mystery of God's love. C. S. Lewis understood the depth of this *mystery* when he wrote: "The command, after all, was 'Take, eat,' not 'Take, understand.'"

Catholics do believe that in the eucharist "the body and blood . . . *the whole Christ is truly, really and substantially* contained" in the consecrated bread and wine (CCC, 1374).

Traditional theology used the word *transubstantiation* to explain the change that takes place in the bread and wine when consecrated, or "made holy," through the actions of the priest, people, and word of God. This means that the substance (the essential reality) of the bread and the substance of the wine are changed into Christ's body and blood, though the externals (taste, appearances, etc.) remain the same.

Catholics base the belief in the real presence on Jesus' own words. For example, in John's gospel, Jesus teaches that we will have no life unless we eat the flesh of the Son of Man and drink his blood. Most of Jesus' listeners could not accept this teaching and left him. The apostles believed and stayed with him (see Jn 6:22ff.). At the Last Supper, Jesus said, "This is my body given for you. . . . This cup is . . . my blood poured out for you" (Lk 22:14-20). St. Paul, the earliest New Testament writer, took these words literally. He warned the Corinthians: "Anyone who eats the bread or drinks the cup of the Lord unworthily is answerable for the body and blood of the Lord" (1 Cor 11:27).

The mystery of the real presence proclaims that our Lord is alive and present in the world, transforming it and us. The church reminds us that Jesus is present to us in many other ways, too. He is present in scripture; the prayer of the church; groups gathered in his name; the poor, sick, and imprisoned; and in all the sacraments (*CCC*, 1373).

The eucharist is the key sacrament. At this celebration, we meet Jesus in the assembled community, in the priest who presides in Jesus' name, in the scriptural word, and—of course—in holy communion. The eucharist is both an invitation and a challenge: We receive Jesus to become Jesus to other people.

20

Why can't non-Catholics receive holy communion at Mass?

The church has very clear guidelines for inter-communion. For non-Catholics to receive holy communion, they must:

- ◆ believe the same as Catholics do about the eucharist

- ◆ be in a state of "urgent necessity" (e.g., in danger of death, facing persecution)

- ◆ be unable to have recourse to their own ministers

- ◆ request the sacrament on their *own* initiative, not at the prompting of a Catholic.

The eucharist is *the* sacrament of faith, unity, and love. Holy communion celebrates the church's unity in the Lord and with each other. It would be false for someone to join in this symbol of unity if he or she does not hold the same beliefs; for example, not believing in the real presence of Christ in the consecrated bread and wine.

For the same reasons the church does not allow Catholics to participate in a communion service at a Protestant service. Receiving communion would imply a unity of belief that does not fully exist. Efforts to repair and reconcile beliefs—known as *ecumenism*—are ongoing between Catholics and Protestants. For now, however, differences in belief remain.

Only the bishop of the local diocese has the authority to judge if inter-communion can take place. Some bishops have given permission for non-Catholic parents to receive holy communion at the marriage of their Catholic children. Others have allowed non-Catholic spouses to receive communion at the funeral of their Catholic husband or wife. These bishops have judged these events (and ones like them) as "urgent needs."

Finally, anyone—Catholic or not—must have the right disposition for eucharist. A person should be in the state of grace, that is, free of any conscious mortal sins. Because the eucharist is a banquet of love, everyone who receives it should do so worthily.

21

I don't get anything out of going to Mass Do I really have to go every Sunday?

Before considering what you "get" out of Mass, you should think about what you give. Our primary motive for going to Mass should be to give not get. We give worship to God by participating in the sacrifice of Jesus which has won us salvation and eternal life. We participate by being attentive, responding, singing, and praying. And the truth of the Mass is that we do get something out of it as well. We "get" the Lord Jesus himself, who loves us beyond compare. This is the greatest gift of all.

Church law holds that Catholics have a serious duty to participate in the Sunday eucharist. Only a valid reason can excuse us from this responsibility, for example, sickness or unusually exhausting work. The reason for the law is because human beings have a natural weakness; we often need external prodding to do right. And, it is right to worship God for one to two hours on Sunday in thanksgiving and praise for the other 167 hours in a week that God gives us. Attending Mass is an act of love to God, our families, our friends, and fellow believers.

People do indeed get bored at Mass. Many activities in life are boring, routine, even difficult. But they are good for us. Eating breakfast day in, day out can be boring, but it is essential to health. Going to school is tough at times, but it is required of you and it pays off. You are to develop your talents so you can prepare for a career and live a full human life.

The question is: Are you a *faithful* Christian? Do you apply the same standard of fidelity to Mass attendance that you do in other areas of your life? Wouldn't you be upset if your car started only three times a week, or the water heater unpredictably dispensed ice cold water, or your computer crashed several times a month? We expect things and other people to be dependable. Doesn't God expect the same from us?

Gale Sayers, a great running back in the 1960s for the Chicago Bears, titled his autobiography *I Am Third*, explaining, "God is first; my family and friends are second; and I am third." Faithful Mass attendance is a way to show where your priorities are. Is God number one in *your* life?

Who's Who of Catholic Church Members

Check the kind of Catholic you expect to be as an adult:

_____ Annuals: can be seen in church in their "Sunday best" on Easter and Christmas only

_____ Leaners: use church for baptisms, weddings, and funerals

_____ Pillars: regular Mass attendees; give support, time, and selves

_____ Specials: help and give on only those occasions that appeal to them

_____ Sponges: take all the church has to give, but never return the favor

_____ Whiners: stay on the outside and criticize and complain about everything

_____ Hypocrites: think they are better than everybody, even the Pillars

What Do You Say?

◆ Should anyone be excluded from the church? Explain.

◆ What would you establish as minimum requirements to be a Catholic?

22

Why do I have to go to confession? I know I'm supposed to go to Mass on Sundays. When am I supposed to go to confession?

Three devils-in-training came up to earth to practice their wiles. Their teacher asked them to describe how they planned to get people to sin. The first said, "I'll use the old method of telling them there is no God, so sin to your heart's delight." The second devil said, "I'll convince them there is no hell, so sin all you want." The third novice, the cleverest of all, responded, "I'll be subtle. I'll tell them, 'Why worry? Sin all you want *now*. You can always repent and be good *later*.'"

Going to confession is a declaration to yourself and to your fellow Christians: "I want to be good—right now!" The sacrament of penance, also known as the sacrament of reconciliation, is Jesus' gift to the church to assure us of his forgiveness and to lighten our hearts.

How often should you go to confession? Church law requires Catholics to confess once a year if they are consciously aware of committing a mortal sin (see Question 32). This law supports another church regulation to receive the eucharist at least once a year, at Easter time. This is a bare minimum for being a practicing Catholic. To receive the eucharist worthily, you should be in a friendship relationship with Jesus, that is, free of mortal sin.

The church recommends regular celebration of this sacrament—for example, during Advent and Lent, on a school retreat, during times of renewal, even every month or so.

Why should you go to confession? Here are some excellent reasons:

💗 **To experience Christ's love firsthand.** Jesus forgave sin. He continues to do so today through his church and his representatives—bishops and priests—to whom he gave power to forgive in his name: "If you forgive anyone's sins, they are forgiven; if you retain anyone's sins, they are retained" (Jn 20:23).

It is very human to want some assurance of love and forgiveness when we have sinned and yet repented. Jesus left this great sign of love to lift our burdens and comfort us.

💗 **To tell the truth about ourselves.** We all sin. We all carry guilt. The New Testament instructs:

If we say, "We have no sin," we are deceiving ourselves, and truth has no place in us; if we acknowledge our sins, he is trustworthy and upright, so that he will forgive our sins and will cleanse us from all evil (1 Jn 1:8-9).

When we confess our sins aloud to Christ's representative, the priest, we overcome self-deception. We have named our sins, a sure sign of contrition and true repentance. Modern psychology tells us that confession is "good for the soul." It lifts burdens, relieves guilt, forgives sin, and starts you on a new path on the spiritual journey.

You should not be afraid to be honest in confession. But if you are, find a sensitive priest and tell him you are nervous. Ask him to help you make a good confession. He'll take it from there. And he will rejoice that you came to him. Remember always that the sacrament of reconciliation is a sacrament of love.

To reconcile with others. Sin is never an isolated affair. It alienates a person from God, self, and others. Confession acknowledges that we need to reconcile ourself to God and to those whom we have harmed. The sacrament of reconciliation heals our sinfulness, repairs our relationship with the Christian community, and challenges us to transform the sinful world in which we live.

To grow in holiness. The sacrament of reconciliation intensifies our love of Jesus. It gives us a more sensitive conscience, so we can look at reality with the eyes of Christ. Going to confession can counteract spiritual laziness and combat bad habits and attitudes. It can draw us closer to God and our brothers and sisters. It can teach us to detest sin and love virtue.

If you have been away from confession for a while, check the times the sacrament is scheduled at your parish and resolve to go. You will be glad you did.

23

My mom and dad have been divorced for over five years. My mom has been miserable ever since. She told me that she can never be married in the church again. Is this true?

Today, divorce touches the lives of almost everyone in our society to a certain degree. You and your family know well the pain divorce causes because you experienced it firsthand.

The understanding of Jesus and the church is that sacramental marriage is a lifelong covenant of love and life between a man and a woman. Fidelity and devoted unconditional love mark this union, one which is fertile ground for raising a Christian family. The church sees in Christian marriage a reflection of Christ's unconditional love for the church and each person.

It is true that the church cannot give permission to a divorced Catholic couple to remarry if they have entered a true, sacramental marriage. This teaching is in obedience to Christ's command not to divorce (see Mt 5:31-32, 19:1-12; Mk 10:11-12; and Lk 16:18) and St. Paul's warning that separated spouses must remain single or reconcile.

You probably know from experience that sometimes it is wise for a couple to separate. Church authorities might even recommend that a couple seek a *civil divorce* to settle child support, custody, property, and alimony issues. But please note: A civil or legal divorce does *not* "dissolve" a valid Christian marriage blessed by God through the church.

The key question in some marriage cases is whether it was a valid Christian sacramental marriage from the beginning. If the answer is "no," the couple can petition for an *annulment* (see Question 24). If the answer is determined to be "yes," then neither husband nor wife can remarry while the other spouse is alive.

Unfortunately one common misunderstanding in years past was that divorced people were not permitted to received the sacraments. This is completely untrue. In fact, the church encourages divorced Catholics to stay close to the Lord and his church. They remain in full communion and can still participate in the eucharist and the sacraments of healing (reconciliation and anointing of the sick) as always. In addition, the church sponsors support groups for the divorced and separated to help them deal with the suffering they are experiencing.

Continue to pray for your mother and father and all who have been touched by divorce. They need your support, love, and understanding.

24

Is an annulment simply a "Catholic divorce" or is it something different?

Sylvestor Stallone, the star of Rocky fame once said: "Boxing is great exercise, as long as you can yell 'cut' whenever you want to."

Some people go into marriage with this same outlook. They don't mind giving it a shot as long as they can "cut out" when they want to. This and similar attitudes show that some persons lacked all understanding of the essence of sacramental marriage or were simply too immature to enter a Christian marriage in the first place. Though they spoke marriage vows that promised lifelong commitment, they were, when reality set in, unwilling to commit themselves to an unconditional relationship. They did not intend to remain married if the going became too rough.

In a decree of nullity the church declares that some essential quality was lacking when a couple exchanged marriage vows. Grounds for a decree of nullity include "lack of form," that is, the marriage did not take place according to church law. Other grounds are lack of knowledge about or reflection on what Christian marriage requires and psychological immaturity by either partner. Pretending to give true consent, hiding an intention never to have children, or inability to complete sexual intercourse are still other grounds for annulment. In short, an annulment says that no marriage really existed.

This is very different from a divorce, that is, a dissolution or breakup of a valid marriage. The church, following the teaching of Christ, does not authorize the dissolution of a valid, consummated, sacramental marriage.

If an annulment is granted, the individuals are free to enter a true Christian marriage in the future.

Christian marriage, because it is such a serious commitment, demands mature preparation and true freedom. Hence, the church insists that a couple should know its requirements *before* getting married.

What Do You Think?

◆ Why do you think there are so many annulments being sought by Catholics today?

25

I can easily worship God on my own. Why do I need the church?

For some people, church comes into their lives only three times: *when hatched, when matched, when dispatched.* At other times, these people either see church as an unnecessary hindrance between God and them or are otherwise too preoccupied to take part.

Also, some people refuse to belong to the church because they equate it with buildings, rules, the hierarchy, or what they term as "phony" members. This is a wrong equation. The church is primarily a *pilgrim people* on a common journey to God. Christians—both saints and sinners—bond together because they know they can't go it alone. Christians need each other to get through life. As the poet John Donne wrote, "No man is an island, entire of itself." Consider these reasons for "needing church":

◆ **The church exists because Jesus founded it.** He wants everyone to belong. Jesus prayed that all people may be one in his name (see Jn 17:20-26). St. Paul termed the church, "the body of Christ," the Lord's presence in the world. Jesus is the head, directing and guiding us, the body, by the power of the Spirit. This means each of us has tremendous worth and dignity with a specific role to play. We are needed in order for the work of Jesus to continue.

◆ **The church gives us the Bible, the good news of Jesus, and guidance on how to live a Christian life.** The Bible was written by Christians who were a part of the Christian community. Its material is meant to guide the church. Church leaders determined what was and was not included.

◆ **We meet Jesus in the church.** The sacraments of the church are grace-filled encounters with the Lord. For example, in the eucharist the Risen Jesus comes to transform us into his disciples and to strengthen us to live the Christian life. Note the meal symbolism. Eating is a joyful, life-sharing act that we do with others. Jesus comes to us in a setting where we are with and care for others.

◆ **Jesus loved associating with ordinary sinners.** It is true that Christians are indeed sinners and hypocrites. Many can also be described as "phony." Jesus came as the divine physician. We all could use a bit of his healing touch. Remember there is no such thing as finding the perfect church.

◆ **Christ continues to guide us in the truth through the pope and bishops.** Complex moral issues confuse today's world. There are many conflicting voices telling us what to think and to do. Thankfully, in Christ's church his voice still speaks the truth to us through the magisterium. Only a person suffering from the moral disease of pride thinks he or she knows it all and can do without help. When you make yourself the church, you choose a fool for a teacher.

However, in the final say, you *can* worship alone. Many people say they'd like to worship God alone in the woods, for example. Unfortunately, they rarely get around to it. But why not worship God alone *and* with others? Enjoy God in nature and enjoy meeting Christ in others through his church.

26

Some people say that all religions are basically the same. On the other hand, my grandfather told me that the Catholic church is the only true church. Which is it?

This question suggests a couple of attitudes we should avoid. First, it is incorrect to say that all religions are the same, teaching only a common version of "do-goodism." Second, it is wrong to insinuate that *all* religious truth belongs to Catholics or, for that matter, any Christian denomination.

A famous story from India illustrates the latter point: Three blind persons are in a dark room groping an elephant. One describes the trunk, another the tail, and a third the feet. All are describing the same reality, but none has a grasp of the entire truth. Religions are like this. Each has a grasp of part of the religious truth, but none can claim to know everything.

Christians would agree with this illustration up to a point. From a Christian perspective, Jesus—the Light of the World—enters the dark room and brings light as well as offering the gift of sight to those who believe in him. This cure is the gift of faith which allows the new Christian to see Christ Jesus as "the Way, the Truth, and the Light" (Jn 14:6). Jesus' presence and the gift of faith enable Christians to comprehend the fullest religious truth that God has revealed to humankind.

If you come to believe that Jesus Christ is God's Ultimate Revealer who saves us, then you must conclude that Christianity is the true religion. Logically, you'd want to join a Christian church.

But *which* Christian church? The Second Vatican Council taught that the church Christ intended to found *subsists* in the Catholic church. This means that *the Catholic church most fully contains and presents Jesus' message.* The traditional four marks of the church help reveal this fullness. Briefly, they show that the church is:

- ◆ *one.* In the Catholic church there is a unity of belief, moral teaching, and liturgical celebration.

- ◆ *holy.* The Catholic church celebrates all seven sacraments—especially the eucharist. It also holds up the Bible, the example of countless saints, many rich prayer styles, and the like, to help a church of sinners strive for holiness.

- ◆ *catholic.* The word *catholic* means "universal." The Catholic church is for all people, in all places, at all times. It is not an exclusive club or limited to certain races, sexes, national or ethnic groups. It is open to everything Jesus taught, and it contains the fullness of a faith relationship to him.

- ◆ *apostolic.* Jesus founded the church on the apostles, who in turn appointed successors. The teaching office of the pope and bishops can be traced back to the apostles. The Catholic church professes the same basic Christian creed first taught by the apostles.

The Catholic church has the fullness of Christ's truth. However, the church also teaches that other Christian churches have varying degrees of sanctification and truth. The Holy Spirit sheds his light and love on other Christian denominations, religions, and indeed all people.

What Do You Say?

◆ C. S. Lewis said Jesus is either "liar, lunatic, or Lord." Choose and defend one of those descriptions.

27
—

Does God save non-Catholics? After all, the majority of people are not Catholic and may not have even heard of Jesus or the church.

God saves all good people. In an eloquent passage, the Second Vatican Council sums up the Catholic response to this question:

> Those can also attain to everlasting salvation who through no fault of their own do not know the gospel of Christ or his church, yet sincerely seek God and, moved by grace, strive by their deeds to do his will as it is known to them through the dictates of conscience. Nor does divine Providence deny the help necessary for salvation to those who, without blame on their part, have not yet arrived at an explicit knowledge of God, but who strive to live a good life, thanks to his grace (*Lumen gentium*, #16).

The church also teaches that the fullest means God intended for our salvation exist in the Catholic church. These means include the seven sacraments, unity in faith, apostolic leadership, and the like (see Question 26). Jesus is the savior of everyone (Acts 4:12), and he is the head of the church, his body. Jesus continues his work of salvation through the church. Thus, those who know that the Catholic church is Christ's church and "refuse to enter her or to remain in her [can]not be saved" *(Lumen gentium, #14).*

However, the church acknowledges that many key elements of salvation, including the work of the Holy Spirit, are present in other churches. This is especially true of Christian churches, but also of Judaism and the great world religions.

God loves everyone, even those who have not heard the gospel or perhaps only have received an incomplete picture of Jesus. St. Paul writes: "God our Savior . . . wants everyone to be saved and reach full knowledge of the truth" (1 Tm 2:3-4). In ways unknown to us, the Spirit moves in the hearts of all. He moves in the depths of their consciences, calling them to do good and avoid evil, and to salvation.

28

More and more it seems as if the media are blatantly anti-Catholic. Why do so many people hate Catholics and the Catholic church?

The Catholic church receives criticism because it goes against the grain of popular society. It is the target of bigotry because it preaches the gospel, stands for absolute values, and represents Christ. As a wise person once said, "You can avoid criticism by saying nothing, doing nothing, and being nothing."

Opposing popular society—being countercultural—will eventually elicit negative comments, even hatred. But this should not surprise us. Jesus himself said that if we want to follow him, we should expect to receive a cross. And, getting this kind of reaction means the church is probably doing something right. Another wise voice said, "It is human to stand with the crowd; it is divine to stand alone."

Certainly, today we do not see the type of widespread discrimination against Catholics that earlier generations experienced. But in recent years, there have been very visible examples of anti-Catholicism. One notorious incident was the mockery of nuns and the crucifix by a Stanford band member at a nationally televised Notre Dame-Stanford football game. Another was the PBS production of a blatantly anti-Catholic film, *Stop the Church.*

More prevalent is the popular media's distorted and unfair profiles of the church and church teaching. Russell Shaw, a Catholic journalist, claims that the media drive the "new" anti-Catholicism by giving preferential coverage to dissenters in the Catholic church. An impartial study—*Media Coverage of the Catholic Church*—documents the media's unfair treatment of official church teaching. If the media are distorting Catholic teaching, we can certainly understand why some people dislike Catholics. Prejudice, after all, is a prejudgment made on insufficient information.

Studies also reveal that most in the media (TV and print reporters, movie producers and actors, and other opinion makers) do not go to church. Rather, they consider themselves "secular humanists" who thumb their noses at religion, with its core belief in the supernatural and a supreme being.

What seems to rankle many of these secularists is the church's strong and consistent stand on issues like abortion, contraception, homosexual lifestyles, and consumerism.

Let's be fair, though. Some of the criticism aimed at the church results from the sins of a few of its most visible members. In recent years, for example, the molesting of children by some priests has received massive media attention. No one can excuse this abuse. It is wrong. It tragically hurts the persons affected. But let us remember that only a very small percentage of people commit these crimes which the media love to sensationalize.

A closing thought: Sailors in the North Sea marvel at how icebergs float in the opposite direction of powerful winds. The reason for this is that eight-ninths of the mass of the typical iceberg is underwater and reacts to the hidden currents. It is like that with the church. The Holy Spirit is guiding the church and helping it to resist—even in the face of criticism—the contrary winds of the modern age.

29

The church is so rich. Why doesn't it sell some of its property and valuables and give more money to the poor?

A long-standing charge, often spread by the enemies of the church, is the so-called wealth of the Catholic church. The church does in fact own many buildings and the property on which they stand, as well as many valuable works of art. Yet this net worth is not liquid, that is, it is not easily converted into cash. Also, those things—buildings, property, and art—are used by the poor and for the poor.

For example, Catholic schools in America are part of the largest private school system in the world, at an enormous savings to tax-payers. Countless hospitals, orphanages, nursing homes, churches to worship in, and similar agencies serve millions of people, many of them poor and non-Catholic. Catholic Charities is the largest charitable organization in the world. Its many agencies directly serve the poor and those on the margins of society.

Vatican City itself is an art museum. People of all faiths can go there to enjoy and appreciate the beautiful achievements of some of humanity's greatest artists. Beautiful cathedrals, priceless art, sculpture, and similar works all over the world give testimony to the human spirit. They are tangible signs of the faith of people whose creative efforts reflect the glory of a brilliant Creator. Humanity would be lacking if the church divested itself of these treasures, which are meant for the ages. Incidentally, someone once estimated that if the church sold all its art works and gave the proceeds to the impoverished, each poor person would receive about 32 cents.

In reality, the Vatican as well as many dioceses around the world are operating at a deficit. In America, Catholics only contribute 1.2 percent of their income to the church, down from 2 percent thirty years ago. The situation is, of course, even more serious in the extreme poverty areas of the world. Your question is a good one, though. Through the ages, some in the church have misused its resources. We cannot excuse these abuses. Jesus identified very strongly with the poor and calls all people to be generous to the poor (see Mt 25). When we respond to the needs of the poor we are responding to Jesus himself. Each of us is a member of Christ's body. St. Ignatius of Loyola stated well the challenge before all Christians:

What have you done for Christ?
What are you doing for Christ?
What will you do for Christ?"

Challenge

- How do you personally respond to the needs of the poor?
- What percentage of your income do you give to the poor?

30

I have a Protestant friend who says unless I am "born again" I can't be saved. What does she mean?

This question comes from an exchange between Jesus and his secret follower, the Pharisee Nicodemus. Jesus said to Nicodemus: "No one can see the kingdom of God unless he is born again" *(Good News Bible).*

Nicodemus did not understand this teaching. He asked Jesus, "Is it possible to go back into the womb again and be born again?" Jesus replied, "In truth I tell you, no one can enter the kingdom of God without being born through water and the Spirit" (Jn 3:3-5).

Catholics interpret this being "born again" as a spiritual rebirth. We believe this takes place at baptism. Baptism gives us the new life of Jesus and the gift of the Holy Spirit, who empowers us to live Christ-like lives.

Various Christian denominations, however, interpret "born again" to be a personal experience that guarantees someone his or her salvation. They often explain this as a specific emotional or spiritual event or an individual private revelation. This experience convinces the person to accept Jesus Christ as a "personal savior." This pivotal event also marks the day on which the person commits his or her life to the Lord. According to this interpretation, if you have this experience, you are saved; if you have not had it, salvation is not yours.

Certainly, some Christians, like St. Paul, do experience the Lord in a way that turns their lives completely around. But having this single experience is *not* a necessary condition for salvation. Rather, the church teaches that baptism begins a new life of spiritual growth. Most often, the Spirit gently leads God's people. Over time, most Christians gradually turn their lives over to Christ. Spiritual rebirth to a life in Christ is another name for Christian conversion. It begins at baptism and signals a lifelong journey of growth. It is not simply a one-time event.

31

—

What is excommunication? For what reasons does a Catholic get excommunicated?

Excommunication is a punishment that excludes a baptized person from being "in communion" with the church, the community of faith. Whenever we sin mortally we suffer a type of excommunication. We cannot fully participate in the life of the Catholic community. The most notable example is how mortal sin prevents us from receiving holy communion until we repent, confess our sin, and firmly resolve to amend our lives.

Excommunication has three purposes: It deters certain actions. It helps people recognize their errors. It calls sinners to repent and reconcile with the church.

One kind of excommunication is *automatic*. It goes into effect as soon as one commits a particular act. The 1983

Code of Canon Law lists the following acts as meriting automatic excommunication:

- desecrating the eucharist

- laying hands violently on the pope

- violating the seal of confession (for priests only)

- giving absolution to an accomplice in sin (for priests only)

- participating in an abortion

- committing the sins of apostasy, heresy, or schism. (According to canon 751: "Apostasy is the total repudiation of the Christian faith." Heresy is the denial of a key truth of faith. Schism is the refusal to submit to the authority of the pope and bishops.)

Another type of excommunication is *imposed* by church authorities; for example, the church would impose excommunication when a non-priest pretends to celebrate the eucharist or pretends to give sacramental absolution.

In general, the church does not publicly announce excommunication. It may do so, however, when a person persists in the action, especially in a public way that gives very bad example to Catholics.

What Do You Say?

Should the church excommunicate politicians who support abortion? Why or why not?

32

___

The meaning of sin and all the different kinds of sin like original sin, mortal sin, and venial sin have always been confusing to me. Can you explain them?

___

Years ago, a *London Times* correspondent, reporting time and again on the bad news of human folly, used to conclude each of his articles with the question, "What's wrong with the world?" The brilliant Catholic convert, G. K. Chesterton, wrote this famous reply:

```
Dear Editor:

"What's wrong with the world?"
I am.
Faithfully yours,
            G.K. Chesterton.
```

His cleverly placed period after "I am" was to show that the root of the world's problems is human sin.

Sin can be defined as *deliberate self-destructiveness that alienates us from God, others, and self.* When we sin, we take a "good" and make it our "god." In the words of St. Augustine, "Sin is believing the lie that you are self-centered, self-dependent, and self-sustained." This distortion of reality causes hurt. We can see this easily when we misuse alcohol, sex, money, power, and the like. Drunkenness, for example, harms a person's body, mind, and spirit as well as his or her relationships with others. All sin is like this.

There are different types and degrees of sin. Theologians distinguish between *original* and *actual sin.* Original sin refers to the very first sin against God, described in the book of Genesis as the deliberate act of disobedience of Adam, the first man. The sin of Adam ruptured the harmonious relationship between God and humankind. This is described as "the fall." Its effects are with us today. Each person is born a sinner, prone to choose evil over good. Thankfully, after the fall, God did not abandon humans once and for all to the power of original sin. Jesus' redemptive sacrifice offers us forgiveness and a rebirth into a new life of grace through the gift of baptism.

Yet, though Christ's life, death, and resurrection conquered original sin and its worst effect—death—humans are still capable of sinning in thoughts, words, deeds, and failures to act. This type of sin is actual sin, that is, personal, individual sin. There are two degrees of actual sin:

- *Venial sin* involves slight matter or does not include one's full consent. A person who commits a venial sin (e.g., telling a white lie) partially rejects God, but does not destroy a friendship relationship with God. The danger with venial sin is that it can dull a person's resolve to the point where his or her relationship with God is neglected. As someone once commented, "The bad thing about little sins is that they grow up too fast."

- *Mortal sin* destroys love and cuts a person off from others and God. It is also called "deadly sin." For a sin to be a mortal sin it must involve serious matter (for example, murder, adultery, blasphemy). The person must also be aware of the seriousness involved and provide full consent of the will. To return to a state of grace and friendship with God a person who has committed a mortal sin must repent and confess his or her sin in the sacrament of reconciliation.

As G. K. Chesterton pointed out, sin is the bad news of what's wrong with the world. The good news to counteract sin is God's forgiveness. Despite our weakness and even our viciousness at times, God's love for us remains constant. We need to acknowledge the truth that we are sinners and turn to the Lord, who will certainly welcome us back. To help remember this, think of this story:

> A teenager told her parish priest that Jesus was appearing to her. To see if the visions were true, the priest said, "Next time Jesus comes, ask him what was my worst sin." Two weeks passed before the teen returned. The priest asked, "Well, what sin did Jesus say I committed?" The young lady answered, "Jesus said he forgot it."

Jesus forgives and forgets. That is the true sign of love for repentant sinners.

33

How do I know if I am doing right?

This question usually involves determining the right way to make a moral decision. To answer, think about some moral decision you want to make. Then ask yourself these questions based on the following categories. They'll help you to know if you are doing right.

The Jesus Test

Is the act loving? Does it serve others or is it self-serving?

The Mother Test

Would you be proud to do this in front of your mother?

The Children Test

Would this action give good example to those younger than you?

The Universal Test

What would happen if you permitted everyone to do this?

The Practicality Test

What will be the results if you do this? Will the consequences be good or bad? Do you have any alternatives to this action? Do you have to do evil to achieve good? (Remember: A good end does not justify evil means to attain it.)

The Integrity Test

Will this make you more honest? Will it strengthen or weaken your character?

The People Test

Will your action treat people as means or ends?

The Bible Test

Does the Bible forbid this action? Specifically, do the Ten Commandments or Christ's law to love God, neighbor, and self forbid it?

The Reality Test

Would a reasonable person do this? If someone asked your advice about this same issue, what would you say?

The Sinner Test

Do you admit that you are weak and may not be

thinking clearly? Is it possible that what you want to do might be wrong? Are your passions getting in the way?

The Prayer Test

Have you asked Jesus for his help? Have you asked the Holy Spirit to enlighten you?

The Church Test

Have you asked a wiser, holier Christian for advice? Have you consulted church teaching on this issue?

Apply these tests and then follow your conscience. If you are honest in how you answer and act on these questions, you are likely to do right.

What Would You Do?

Apply the tests in Question 33 to the following situations:

✘ stealing supplies from work

✘ gossiping about a classmate's sexual orientation

✘ cheating on a quiz

✘ consuming a couple of beers before going to a football game

✘ making racist comments to a member of a minority

✘ pressuring a date for sex

✘ using obscene language

34

What does it mean to "follow your conscience?" Must I always follow my conscience?

A teacher asked a precocious sixth-grader if he knew the difference between the words *conscious* and *conscience*. "Yes," replied the boy. "Conscious means 'being aware of something.' Conscience is wishing you weren't."

By definition, conscience is the practical judgment about the rightness or wrongness of an action or attitude. It is the ability to discover God's will for your life. Your conscience enables you to hear God's voice speak to your heart.

Babe Didrikson Zaharias, a great golfer of the 1950s, exemplified a mature conscience. She once disqualified herself from a tournament because she hit the wrong ball out of the rough. "But nobody would have known," a friend told her. "I would have known," she replied.

The measure of a person's character is what he or she or he would do if no one would ever find out.

The Catholic church teaches two important rules about conscience:

1. Always form your conscience.

2. Always follow your conscience.

Forming one's conscience is a serious responsibility. For a Catholic, this is a lifelong task that takes place within the Christian community. The scriptures and the church's magisterium ("teaching office") are two key sources of authentic truth about right and wrong. Jesus empowered Peter, the apostles, and their successors (the pope and bishops) to teach and interpret his word and truth in the area of faith and morals. When we listen to the church's official teachers, we are in effect listening to Christ (Lk 10:16).

Everyone must obey his or her conscience. It is the subjective norm of morality. Note, though, that conscience is one's *own* judgment. Thus, it can be wrong. People can make mistakes because, through no fault of their own, they may not know that certain actions or attitudes are destructive. Ignorance in cases like this is not blameworthy. But negligence, selfishness, prejudice, or laziness cannot excuse an ill-informed conscience.

Yes, to answer your second question, you must follow your conscience. But to do so well you must always form it by learning from and assenting to Christ's teaching as it comes to us in the church.

35

I know some people who play around with ouija boards and others who are into astrology. My mom told me these things are associated with the occult. What does she mean?

The *occult* has to do with things that are "hidden" or "concealed." "Occultism" tries to invoke superhuman—not divine—powers to reveal or control the future. It involves several practices:

- *Superstition* invests godlike powers in ordinary things.
- *Astrology* tries to learn about the future from the stars.

- *Divinization* communicates with hidden forces, considered evil by the church, to learn about the future. Common practices of divinizers today include reading Tarot cards and palms, using ouija boards, and consulting fortunetellers.

- *Spiritism* tries to contact the dead through mediums and seances.

The Bible severely condemns as gravely wrong all of these occult practices (see, for example, Dt 18:10-14 and Lv 20:27). The church also has consistently outlawed these occult activities. According to the *Catechism of the Catholic Church*: "They contradict the honor, respect, and loving fear that we owe to God alone" (2116).

Occult practices are a form of *idolatry*, that is, worshiping and trusting a false god. Occultism denies that Jesus is the source of knowledge. It represents a profound lack of trust in God. The *Catechism of the Catholic Church* also teaches that a sound Christian attitude consists in putting oneself confidently into the hands of Providence for whatever concerns the future, and giving up all unhealthy curiosity about it (2115).

One final word about these practices. Those who dabble in the occult are vulnerable to other "gods" that seek to dominate their lives. These include the "gods" of money, power, sex, drugs, and even, tragically, Satan, himself.

Listen to your mom. Convince your friends to avoid occult practices at all costs. And commit yourself to trusting and loving God above all else.

*N*ow the Spirit explicitly says that in the last times some will turn away from the faith by paying attention to deceitful spirits and demonic instructions.

~1 Timothy 4:1, NAB

36

—

There are worse things to do than drinking a few beers or smoking pot. What's the harm in occasionally getting high?

Consider the lesson of an old story: "Alcohol makes you more colorful. It give you a red nose, a white liver, a yellow streak, and a blue outlook." Alcohol, though, is not evil in itself. Jesus himself drank it. His first miracle was to change water into wine at a wedding (Jn 2). He used wine, along with bread, when he gave us the eucharist.

The trouble with alcohol is not with its use, but its misuse. It is especially easy to abuse alcohol because it is an addictive substance. Hence, it is hard to be a person who only "occasionally gets high." The same reasoning is true of marijuana, a hallucinogenic drug. The body builds a tolerance to marijuana as a person uses it more often, leading one to require stronger doses to get high as well as to a psychological dependence on the drug.

The pattern for teens who become dependent on alcohol and/or other drugs usually goes like this: Peer pressure leads a teen to get high for a first time. An alcohol high lowers inhibitions. Marijuana may cause giddiness. This "fun" leads the person to try the experience again. A pattern has been established, even if the experience of being high never again meets the person's expectations and leaves the person depressed once the effects of the drug wear off.

Alcohol and drug abuse lead to tragedy. This is why parents and schools make so much effort to dissuade you from using them. You are likely aware of many of the facts. For example, alcohol figures in half of all car and fire accidents, two-thirds of all murders, and one-third of suicides.

It causes more than 200,000 deaths annually. Add in other drugs and the figures are even higher. There are several other dangers of alcohol and marijuana use, including:

- *Physically*, alcohol damages the liver, stresses the heart, impairs memory, and often creates the need for a greater amount or tempts one to try a stronger drug. Marijuana use leads to lung cancer and prevents the proper formation of DNA, proteins, and other essentials for cell growth and cell division.

- *Emotionally*, alcohol and marijuana use cause guilt, a poor self-image, and embarrassment over stupid behavior done under their influence.

- *Socially*, alcohol is a factor in family problems like domestic violence, broken homes, assaults, and even murder. Marijuana use causes people to lose interest in things that were once important to them.

- *Legally*, especially for teens, alcohol and marijuana use involves deception and disregard for the law.

- *Psychologically*, any drug use encourages immaturity and immediate gratification. Though alcohol and marijuana seem to provide a temporary escape from problems, one learns quickly that the problems never go away by themselves, and may be compounded by the use of alcohol and marijuana.

- *Spiritually*, alcohol and marijuana use limit freedom and dull one's ability to think. They make it hard to choose right from wrong, for example, in the area of sexual morality.

One can safely say that misuse of these substances is suicide on the installment plan. You should think about all the factors of alcohol and drug use *before* endangering yourself and others.

---

*W*ine is reckless, liquor rowdy;

unwise is anyone whom it seduces.

What Do You Say?

Share a realistic strategy to resist peer pressure to use alcohol or other drugs.

37

I am unclear of the church's pro-life stance. Why doesn't the church allow for abortion in cases like rape and incest or when the pregnancy threatens the life of the mother?

The bottom line is that it is not right deliberately to kill an unborn child under any circumstances. Each human being, made in God's image and likeness, is a precious person of dignity. No human life, even unborn human life conceived in the worst of circumstances, is ours to do with as we please. Human life is God's. Helpless, unborn human beings especially need reverence and protection.

Ask yourself the question, "Was the baby at fault in the rape or incest cases?" Though the baby comes into the world through tragic circumstances, it is not to blame for those circumstances. The baby and victim of rape or incest are innocent. Each deserves the complete support and love of the community in this emotionally devastating time. Christians do what is right when they care for these innocent babies as well as the female victims of male violence.

Next, consider the case of a difficult pregnancy which threatens the life of the mother. (Note that these cases are extremely rare in modern medicine. Modern medical skills and procedures have developed to such a degree that doctors can almost always save both mother and baby.) Though it is never right directly to kill an innocent baby, Catholic moral theology *permits* the death of a baby when it is the indirect result of a life-saving operation for the mother.

A classic, but once again extremely rare, example is the case of a mother with a cancerous uterus. If the only way to save the mother's life is to remove the uterus, even if the non-viable fetus would die in the process, then the procedure would be permissible. Note in this example there is no direct attack on the baby. One does not intend the death of the baby. It is a last-resort procedure to save the mother. These conditions would make this extremely rare procedure permissible.

In conclusion, the church's position on abortion is extremely clear: It is right to protect the life of innocent unborn human beings, no matter how they were conceived. Abortion—the deliberate killing of unborn human life—is wrong regardless of the circumstances. As Pope John Paul II has written in his important encyclical *The Gospel of Life:*

I confirm that the direct and voluntary killing of an innocent human being is always gravely immoral. . . .

T he deliberate decision to deprive an innocent human being of his life is always morally evil and can never be licit either as an end in itself or as a means to a good end. . . .

A s far as the right to life is concerned, every innocent human being is absolutely equal to all others (#57).

C owardice asks the question, "Is it safe?" Expedience asks the question, "Is it politic?" Vanity asks the question, "Is it popular?" But conscience asks the question, "Is it right?"

~Martin Luther King, Jr.

38

A girl I know had an abortion. Is she kicked out of the church forever? What should she do?

Your questions reveal that you realize the seriousness of abortion. The church underscores its gravity by imposing automatic excommunication on anyone who takes part in an abortion (see Question 31). However, certain conditions must be present.

For example, the woman must be 18 years old and aware that excommunication is the penalty for abortion. Second, the woman must freely choose to abort her baby. Women who have abortions are often profoundly afraid, confused, and under severe pressure (from family, the man involved, and her friends). If any of these conditions is present at the time of an abortion, then she does not incur automatic excommunication.

Thus, it is unlikely that a teenage girl who secured an abortion has been "kicked out of the church." But she has committed an offense that objectively involves the most "serious matter"—the taking of human life. Depending on the degree of freedom and knowledge of wrongdoing, she may be guilty of mortal sin.

Her first step is to admit that she has sinned. Pope John Paul II offers some sensitive and consoling words to women who have had abortions:

> *C*ertainly what happened was and remains terribly wrong. But do not give in to discouragements and do not lose hope. Try rather to understand what happened and face it honestly. If you have not already done so, give yourselves over with humility and trust to repentance. The Father of mercies is ready to give you his forgiveness and peace in the sacrament of reconciliation. You will come to understand that nothing is definitively lost, and you will also be able to ask forgiveness from your child, who is now living in the Lord (*The Gospel of Life, #99*).

Repentance is indeed the beginning of the healing process. Jesus forgives all repentant sinners, no matter how grave the offense. If the girl you know asks for your help or advice, remind her of God's willingness to forgive all people of their sins. Share with her the parable of the Prodigal Son (Lk 15:11-32), which stresses God's unconditional love for those who have strayed. Encourage her to reconcile with God and the Christian community in the sacrament of reconciliation. A sensitive confessor will repeat the message of God's love and advise her on what to do next. For example, he will probably recommend that she receive some follow-up counseling. The church sponsors counseling through a group called Project Rachel.

Like a loving mother, the church has open arms for this girl. May you help her to feel willing and able to seek reconciliation and healing.

For Reference

Contact a local Catholic church for the phone number and address of the Project Rachel ministry near you, or you may contact the national office:

Project Rachel
National Office of Post Abortion Reconciliation and Healing
3501 South Lake Drive
Milwaukee, WI 53207
1-800-5-WECARE

39

Why is the church against birth control?

Your question brings up a common misstatement of the church's position. The church is against *artificial* birth control; it does teach that parents must exercise human and Christian responsibility in planning and raising a family. A husband and wife, in dialogue with each other and with God, will consider their physical and psychological health, family finances, and present family size in responsibly planning their family. God does not require a couple to have as many children as possible. In most cases, doing so would be irresponsible.

Thus, the church does encourage family planning out of unselfish motives using natural and moral means. The church approves the Natural Family Planning methods of birth control to determine the spacing and number of children in a family. These methods are called "natural" because the couple does not use anything mechanical or artificial (e.g., a condom or birth control pills). Natural Family Planning depends on a woman charting her fertility cycle and she and her husband abstaining from sexual intercourse during those days of the cycle when the wife can conceive a child.

The definitive teaching on responsible transmission of human life appears in Pope Paul VI's encyclical *Humanae Vitae* (1968). The pope noted that sexual intercourse in marriage has two purposes: unitive (the sharing of love) and procreative (the giving of life). In order for sexual intercourse to conform to God's plan, it must be in harmony with *both* purposes: "Each and every marriage act must remain open to the transmission of life" (*Humanae Vitae*,

#11). Artificial means of birth control unnaturally frustrate one of the purposes of marriage, the procreative dimension. Thus, they are wrong.

In a society that promotes self-indulgence, it is a challenge for Catholic couples to live in harmony with God's design for sexual intercourse in marriage. The church, however, offers its compassion and concern to couples struggling to do right in the area of family planning. Couples are reminded to celebrate the sacraments frequently and to engage in honest self-reflection, prayer, and meditation on the reasons behind church teaching.

40
—

Is Natural Family Planning really an effective way to plan pregnancies?

Many married couples—Catholic and otherwise—are finding that Natural Family Planning (NFP) is a highly effective means of regulating birth. It has a 98 percent effective rate in regulating pregnancy if practiced correctly. But it has many other benefits as well. For example, it improves communication between the husband and wife. Abstaining from sexual intercourse for a few days also helps the couple appreciate and enjoy their love-making even more.

When a couple uses artificial means of birth control they are holding something back. Sexual sharing is meant to express *total* self-giving. Because NFP is in harmony with God's plan, the husband and wife really make a *total* gift of themselves to each other. According to the *Catechism of the Catholic Church:*

*P*eriodic continence, that is, the methods of birth regulation based on self-observation and the use of infertile periods, is in conformity with the objective criteria of morality. These methods respect the bodies of the spouses, encourage tenderness between them, and favor the education of an authentic freedom *(CCC, 2370)*.

How does NFP work? A few basic facts first. Normally, an ovum (egg) is released from a woman's ovary about fourteen days before menstruation. It lives for about twenty-four hours after its release. This twenty-four-hour period is when fertilization (pregnancy) can occur, if the male's sperm unites with the ovum. Typically, the sperm can live around seventy-two hours. Thus, for roughly four days out of each regular menstrual cycle, pregnancy can happen.

NFP helps the couple determine when the fertile times take place. (Admittedly this is more difficult for women who do not have a regular twenty-eight day cycle.) The wife daily examines the thickness and color of her cervical mucus. This examination helps her determine the fertile period. The couple also keeps a chart that tracks her cycle. This aids communication and helps the husband and wife determine when they should refrain from sex. But it also helps them determine the best time to have intercourse when they want to have a child.

For Reference

A helpful resource on NFP is called *The Art of Natural Family Planning*. It is available from:

Couple-to-Couple League
P.O. Box 11184
Cincinnati, OH 45211

41

—

I wouldn't cheat on tests and schoolwork if everyone else didn't. But I do cheat because I don't want to fall behind. What's so bad about a little cheating?

In recent years "a hole in the moral ozone" has been discovered. For example, a recent survey determined that one in eight college students admits to committing fraud, like lying on financial aid forms and borrowing money with no intention to pay it back. Also, most high-school and college students admit to cheating on exams.

Cheating is wrong because it involves deception and theft. Cheaters take what doesn't belong to them (a violation of the seventh commandment, which forbids stealing). Then, they pass it off as their own (a violation of the eighth commandment, which forbids false witness).

The trouble with even "a little cheating" is drawing the line. If you cheat in little things often enough, you next are likely to cheat in bigger things. Then you actually are a cheater. Soon your conscience dulls and you will think nothing of making excuses for cheating in all areas of your life. Sin is like that. It starts small, pokes a hole in the "moral ozone," and then pretty soon allows for the justification of anything, right or wrong.

Honesty is the touchstone of a person's character. To the degree that you are honest and willing to stand alone you are a person of integrity. In a world that tolerates deception in politicians, infidelity in marriage, and inferior workmanship, it takes moral courage to be honest and resist the crowd.

Jesus can help you be a person of integrity. There is a story about the local butcher whose life turned around when he decided to follow Jesus. "I stopped weighing with my thumb," he said. "Before I met Christ, I placed my thumb on the scale in a way that added an ounce to the weight of the meat. Now that I am following Christ I use the scale correctly. I am also making restitution to all the customers I have cheated in the past."

Do yourself a favor and say "no" to cheating. Perhaps you can adopt for your own West Point's "Cadet Prayer." The cadets recite these words every Sunday:

> *M*ake us choose the harder right instead of the easier wrong, and never be content with half truth when whole truth can be won. Endow us with courage that is born of loyalty to all that is noble and worthy, that scorns to compromise with vice and injustice and knows no fear when right and truth are in jeopardy.

What Do You Say?

- Right or wrong? I tell people what they want to hear rather than what I really believe. Explain.

- Right or wrong? I have my mom call school to say I am sick when I really just want to stay home to finish a term paper. Explain.

- Right or wrong? I do not correct the waitress who mistotaled the bill in my favor. Explain.

- Right or wrong? I make personal phone calls while on the job. Explain.

Why does God allow for evil and suffering in the world?

How can a good and loving God send someone to hell? This doesn't sound very loving to me.

How ca___ __ th__ t_ b_ f__ if G_d _____ _ _____ thing t__ _____ _____ ___ __ the future?

Did Jesu_ _____

The chu___ _____ _____ _____ yet the _____ _____ _____ sisters."

Some p____ _____ _____ _____ he at le____ _____ _____ people?

How ca___

What _____ _____ come fr____

My you____ _____ "Cathol__ _____ Bibles _

Was th____ _____

Do miracles happen today?

Does Satan really exist?

Why do we have to die?

What is reincarnation? What does the church teach about reincarnation?

Chapter

3

God Writes Straight with Crooked Lines

Mysteries of the Bible, Jesus, and Life

*L*ife is full of mysteries. Some are pleasant, for example, our wonderment as we ponder a life of peace and joy in eternity. Others are more confusing; we may wonder how a good and loving God can allow evil and suffering. The philosopher Friedrich Nietzsche would have us ask these questions:

*A*re you one who looks on? Or one who lends a hand? Or one who looks away and walks off?

Do you want to walk along? Or walk ahead? Or walk by yourself?

One must know *what* one wants and *that* one wants.[1]

How do you answer these questions? Certainly, Jesus knew *that* he wanted, and his life proved *what* he wanted: the redemption of us, those he called friends.

In this chapter, we will wrestle with some of the tough questions about life, God, Jesus, and the Bible. Although we cannot perfectly grasp every mystery these questions raise, we can surely come to know as a friend the One who lent a hand and who led the way to our salvation.

42

Why does God allow for evil and suffering in the world?

This question has challenged all religions, including Christianity, from time immemorial.

For example, in the Old Testament, the book of Job wrestles with this same problem. Job was a good man who lost all his children and property and contracted a horrible disease. Always trusting God despite his setbacks, Job's sufferings revealed one partial answer to why there is suffering: Good can come from it. Job became a more holy man, a better friend, and more trusting of God because of his sufferings. The story of Joseph in Genesis 37—45 also points this out. Joseph was shoved into a ditch and left for dead by his brothers. Yet from this suffering he emerged as the pharaoh's assistant in Egypt, in charge of dispensing food during a worldwide famine. In this position he was able to save his own family from starvation.

A key insight of Job came toward the end of his trials. Job says to God:

You have told me about great works that I cannot understand, about marvels which are beyond me, of which I know nothing . . . but now, having seen you with my own eyes, I retract what I have said, and repent in dust and ashes (Jb 42:3, 5-6).

Job admits that God's ways are mysterious and that ultimately we can't understand them. It takes humility and trust to admit that we can never completely understand the mystery of innocent suffering and evil in the world.

But we can understand some things about evil and suffering. Consider these points:

- *God's created world is on a journey to perfection.* The world is in a process of becoming. It is not yet perfect. Nature's constructive and destructive forces exist side-by-side. The more perfect exists alongside the less perfect: "With physical good there also exists physical evil as long as creation has not reached perfection" (CCC, 310).

   Just as the star athlete must experience the pain that accompanies training to hone his or her skills, so the world undergoes pain to achieve the perfection God has in store. We cannot now appreciate the pain involved in this growth process because innocent people suffer at the hands of nature. But we believe that in God's wisdom this growth is good for both individuals and humanity as a whole as we journey to perfection.

- *The misuse of freedom is the cause of much moral evil.* Out of divine goodness, God created humans (and angels) as *intelligent* and *free* creatures, not mere automatons. But these two gifts require responsibility. We must freely choose to love God and others on our journey toward eternity. When we refuse to love, we sin. And sin brings about incredible evil and suffering.

Christian revelation tells us that when some angels chose to sin, they (fallen angels, or devils) unleashed evil in the world in opposition to God. This is one explanation of some of the natural evil in the world (e.g., tornadoes, earthquakes, and the like).

Human sin leads to moral evils like war, rape, abortion, drug abuse, prejudice, and greed. God does not *cause* moral evil. Humans, by misusing their freedom, are the cause. God *permits* moral evil, however, because God loves and respects the free creatures he has made. And in a way known only to God (a truth that Job eventually admitted), God knows how to derive good out of all evil.

- *Christian faith announces the good news of Jesus Christ, who conquered the forces of evil.* Certainly, the worst moral evil in the world was for humans to put to death the innocent God-man. Like any normal person, Jesus abhorred suffering and even asked his Father to remove it. But Jesus freely embraced the sufferings that unjustly came his way by submitting to his Father, "May your will be done."

God heard Jesus' prayer, not by saving Jesus from death, but by saving him *out* of death. Jesus' suffering, death, and resurrection have conquered the worst evil: death and separation from God. If we love as Jesus teaches us to do and join our sufferings to him, we will share forever in the Lord's blissful, superabundant, joy-filled life.

This is "good news" that can help us cope with the mystery of evil and suffering.

*C*onsider the work of God. Who can make straight what he has made crooked? On a good day enjoy good things, and on an evil day consider: Both the one and the other God has made, so that man cannot find fault with him in anything.

~Ecclesiastes 7:13-14 (NAB)

What Do You Think?

When was a time some good came out of an "evil" that befell you.

43

How can a good and loving God send someone to hell? This doesn't sound very loving to me.

We can make three points to support a loving God who allows free creatures to choose a path that leads either to heaven or perdition:

1. God *"wants everyone to be saved"* (1 Tm 2:4). As the New Testament teaches, the Lord is "patient with you, wanting nobody to be lost and everybody to be brought to repentance" (2 Pt 3:9).

2. *God gives all people countless opportunities to repent of their sins, to accept truth and love.* The Lord is free with his gifts. The graces to live a good life are always present to everyone throughout life. A person can accept

these graces or reject them; everyone is free to make his or her own choice.

Thus, there won't be surprises at judgment time. We will know what kind of life we chose and what we deserve as reward. God is not "out to get us," to catch us in some failing, zap us, or condemn us to eternal hell. God is the loving Father of the parable of the Prodigal Son. God always awaits repentant sinners with open arms. Why blame God if a person repeatedly chooses to turn away from this love?

3. *A true sign of love is that it allows people freedom, even if the possibility exists that the freedom will lead the person to do harmful, even self-destructive things.* God so loves us that we are entrusted with that kind of freedom.

You may ask yourself, is it more loving for God to create free, intelligent beings who can respond in love or mere robots who have no freedom? Compare God to your parents. As you mature, they risk giving you increasing amounts of freedom so you can responsibly become an adult. Would they really love you if they never allowed you to do anything? Would you ever be your own person? Obviously, the answer is no. You would likely endure a boring, unproductive, and unhappy life.

In truth, God doesn't condemn anyone to hell. People themselves choose their own destiny by the decisions they make.

Heaven or Hell?

Heaven and hell are the same place—a wonderful banquet hall where people gather around a table overflowing with the most delectable food. They can't wait to enjoy the feast.

owever, there is one condition. Each person must eat with an eight-foot spoon. The people in heaven are deliriously happy while those in hell are frustrated and eternally unhappy. Why? Well, those in hell are so accustomed to living in greed that they unsuccessfully try to feed themselves— an impossible task with an eight-foot spoon. Those in heaven, in contrast, eat to their hearts' content because they feed those across the table with their over-sized spoons! They've learned to care for others. And their reward is eternal happiness.

44

How can people be truly free if God knows everything that is going to happen to them in the future?

God is indeed *omniscient*, that is, "all-knowing." God knows all that happens, has happened, and will happen. In addition, God endows people with an intellect and a free will. Your free will enables you to choose. And your choices are real, not illusions. Also, God has created a world with natural laws (e.g., the law of gravity). Ordinarily God does not interfere with these laws of nature.

God's knowing everything does not take away your freedom. For example, God knows you will sin. Sin is contrary to God's will. But God permits you to sin because God respects your use of free will. Obviously, God wants you to choose love, the life of God. But God doesn't force you to love. The nature of love is to allow the other to be free. And God is Love. Remember, though, that God will always forgive you when you are sorry for your misuse of freedom.

Let's take two examples to help you see how God's omniscience interacts with your gift of freedom.

In the first, a group of teens, out drinking all night, decides to drive home. The driver, under the influence of alcohol, crashes the car into a tree. Did God *know* this would happen? Yes. Did God *permit* this to happen? Yes, because God respects our free will and ordinarily does not suspend the laws of nature (for example, by moving the tree to avoid the car). Did God *cause* the accident? No, an abuse of human freedom caused it—getting intoxicated, driving under the influence of alcohol, and driving reck-lessly. God did not foreordain the teens to drink. God's knowledge did not take away their power to act freely. They could have chosen otherwise.

In the second example, you are looking out of a win-dow on the fifth floor of a building. You see a car speeding to an intersection. You know it will hit a pedestrian who is looking in the opposite direction. Unfortunately, the car does strike the inattentive person. Your foreknowledge did not *cause* the accident. God's omniscience works like this.

45

—

Did Jesus know he was God?

Before tackling this fascinating question, we should note several points. First, the gospels are virtually our only source of knowledge about the historical Jesus. Second, the purpose of the gospels is to inform us "what *we* should know about Jesus, not what he knew about himself."[2] Third, the gospels do not give us access to what went on in Jesus' mind. Apparently, Jesus did not share his intimate thoughts on his self-identity as he grew up in Nazareth. Many of his neighborhood friends and relatives, for example, thought he was pretty ordinary. And once he began his preaching and healing ministries, some even thought he was crazy! (See, for example, Mk 3:21 and 6:2-3.)

Fr. Raymond Brown, a prominent scripture scholar, does not like the phrasing of the question, "Did Jesus know he was God?" For a first-century Jew, *God* meant the One who dwells in the heavens. If asked if he were God in this sense, Jesus would have said "no" because he—Jesus—was visibly present on earth. To illustrate this point, consider Jesus' response as recorded in the gospel of Mark, the earliest gospel written (approximately A.D. 60-65) when someone addressed Jesus as "good teacher." Jesus said, "Why do you call me good? No one is good but God alone" (Mk 10:17-18).

However, in John's later gospel (written in the 90s), Thomas calls Jesus "my Lord and my God" (Jn 20:28) and is affirmed in doing so. What happened in the years between the writing of Mark and John? Undoubtedly, the early Christian community, under the direction of the Holy Spirit, grew to realize that the word "God" applied not only to the Father in heaven, but to the Son on earth. The early Christians came to understand that Jesus is so intimately related to God that they could rightly call him God as well. Jesus did not change, but the understanding of the early Christians about Jesus did.

Brown believes a better way to phrase the question is: "Did Jesus know that he had an identity which his followers later came to understand in terms of being God? If he was God ... did he know who he was?"[3] The answer is yes! Here is some evidence to support this conclusion:

- There is no scene in the gospels where Jesus discovers something new about himself. He always knew who he was.

- Jesus claimed a unique relationship with his Abba-Father. Many Jews believed he was indeed professing to be on a par with Yahweh, the God of their history. In fact, the authorities charged Jesus with blasphemy: "Though you are only a man, you claim to be God" (Jn 10:33).

- Jesus certainly must have known his identity, since he taught with awesome authority. For example, he claimed to forgive sin, something only God can do. To prove he had the power to forgive sin, and thus reveal his true identity, Jesus performed a miracle (Mk 2:3-12). This validated his claim.

- Jesus said many other things which in effect tell us that he knew who he was. For example, he claimed to be Lord of the Sabbath (Mt 12:8), to be greater than the Law (Mt 5:27-28), to be above the angels (Mt 13:41), and to be equal to God (Mt 11:27).

46

The church teaches that Mary was "ever virgin," yet the Bible says that Jesus had "brothers and sisters." How can both be true?

This question arises out of passages in the New Testament (most notably, Mt 13:55-56, Mk 6:1-6) that refer to certain "brothers and sisters" of Jesus. Catholics have always believed that these so-called brothers and sisters of Jesus were actually his cousins or other close relatives. Hence, the church continues its long-standing belief that Mary was "ever virgin."

This traditional belief rests on the solid research of scripture scholars. They conclude that neither Hebrew nor the western Aramaic language that Jesus spoke had a special word meaning "cousin." The patriarchal family dominated Jesus' world. His society considered the oldest living male—the patriarch—the father. In such a family, relatives, like cousins, referred to themselves as brothers and sisters.

Patriarchal families exist even today. A Jesuit friend of mine told me of his missionary days in Nepal. He would often have in class two students with the same surname. When my friend asked the boys if they were brothers, they often said "yes." Only after some months did my friend learn that most of these "brothers" were really cousins. In reality, their fathers were brothers. And because of the closeness of their families, the two boys—actually cousins—considered themselves brothers.

Scripture gives even more support to the church's interpretation. For example, two of the men Matthew's gospel names as brothers of Jesus—James and Joset—could not have been the sons of Mary, Jesus' mother, because Matthew (27:56) and Mark (15:40) mention them as the sons of another Mary. This Mary was one of the women who witnessed Jesus' crucifixion and who later went to anoint him on Easter Sunday morning.

Finally, consider this question: If Jesus had blood brothers, why would he entrust the care of his mother Mary to John, the beloved disciple, and not to one of his so-called siblings (Jn 19:26)?

47

—

Some people say Jesus was married. Was he? Did he at least experience sexual desires like other people?

We live in a sex-obsessed age which preaches that an active sex life is the be-all and end-all of human existence. But when we read the New Testament, we see that Jesus rarely speaks about sex. He cares more about respect in human relationships. In first-century Palestine, men looked on women as objects they owned, as outlets for their own pleasure. They could toss their wives aside for virtually any reason. In contrast, Jesus taught that men should treat women with courtesy and respect. His own example elevated the role of women: he condemned lust, adultery, and divorce.

Scripture and the early church councils teach that Jesus is like us in everything but sin. Therefore, as a teen and a young man, Jesus had to learn to integrate his maturing sexuality into his personality as anyone else would. However, unlike most, he did so without disrespecting self or others, that is, without sin.

As for the question of whether Jesus was married, the church has always taught that Jesus *never* married. The main evidence for this teaching is that nowhere in the gospel is there any mention of a wife or children of Jesus. The gospels do name Jesus' mother, his foster father, his so-called brothers, his close male apostles and disciples, his cousin John the Baptist, and various women disciples like Mary Magdalene, Salome, the sisters Mary and Martha, and others. It would be very strange for the gospel writers never to even hint that Jesus had a wife and children, if in fact he did.

Though it was very much the norm for young Jewish men of Jesus' day to marry by the time they were eighteen years old, there were some men who took the vow of celibacy. For example, a Jewish sect known as the Essenes lived a strict life of prayer, fasting, and celibacy in the desert.

There is no doubt that Jesus loved married people and children. His first miracle in John's gospel took place at a wedding feast at Cana. Tradition holds that all the apostles except John were married. And Jesus loved being with children.

We can speculate that Jesus did not marry because his passionate, all-consuming vocation was to proclaim and spread God's kingdom. In Matthew 19:12 Jesus refers to those who make themselves eunuchs for the sake of God's kingdom. Jesus calls this a gift that some will freely choose in order to further God's work. Undoubtedly, Jesus himself chose this path.

What Do You Think?

If you could ask Jesus any one question, what would it be?

48

How can Jesus be both God and human?

Imagine, if you can, a mere thimble holding all the oceans of the world. This is incredible when you think about it. How could a mere thimble contain an almost infinite amount of water? But this example pales in comparison to our belief in the Incarnation, the doctrine that in Jesus Christ the immensity and boundlessness of God took human form in order to save us.

Christianity professes that Jesus of Nazareth, a historical person who lived and died and walked the earth is also the Second Person of the Blessed Trinity. Thus, Jesus, one divine person, has both a divine nature and a human nature. He is completely God; at the same time, he is completely human.

How this can be is a mystery of love beyond human comprehension. If we could understand how Christ could be both God and human, Jesus would be no greater than us. But we accept it as true because God has given us the gift of faith and the grace to believe it. The gift of the Incarnation also helps us understand so many other truths about God and about our own human destiny.

For example:

- *We have been created precious in God's sight.* We can proclaim with great pride, "He was one of us." Jesus is our Lord, our savior, and our brother. St. Athanasius said, "The Word was not degraded by receiving a body. . . . Rather he deified what he put on; and, more than that, he bestowed this gift upon [us]."

  The Incarnation teaches that we are beings of tremendous worth and dignity. Jesus, our brother, adopts us into the divine family.

- *Jesus shows us the way to live.* His life is the model for all to follow. His suffering and death graphically demonstrate the meaning of love. He practiced what he preached. Because he is one of us, he completely understands what we are going through and is thus completely willing to lend us his support and grace. He typifies the meaning of a true friend.

- *God loves us with an infinite love.* Not only did God take human form, but he gave his life for us. An early Christian hymn puts it this way:

Who, being in the form of God,
did not count equality with God
something to be grasped.

But emptied himself,
taking the form of a slave,
becoming as human beings are;
and being in every way like a human being,
he was humbler yet,
even to accepting death, death on a cross
                    ~Phillippians 2:6-8

Jesus' death and resurrection bring forgiveness for our sins and make it possible for us to live forever! Is there greater love? Is there better news?

In the beginning was the Word:
the Word was with God
and the Word was God.
Through him all things came into being . . .
The Word became flesh,
he lived among us. . . .
                    ~John 1:1, 3, 14

Checklist

Check any statements about Jesus that you agree with.

_____ Jesus is the Messiah.

_____ Jesus is my best friend.

_____ Jesus is my brother.

_____ Jesus is fully human.

_____ Jesus is fully God.

_____ Jesus is my personal savior.

_____ Jesus is the "Truth."

_____ Jesus lives!

_____ Jesus is the Second Person of the Trinity.

_____ Jesus is my Lord.

Why do you respond the way you did to each item?

49

What makes the Bible so special? Where did it come from?

The Bible is unlike any other book. Whereas we look to most books for *information*, we look to the Bible for *transformation*. The following story illustrates this well:

A South Sea Islander proudly showed his bible to an American soldier during World War II. "Oh, we stopped reading that long ago," the soldier said.

The native, once a cannibal, smiled back, "It's good we haven't. If it weren't for this book, you'd have been a meal by now."

The word bible comes from the Greek *biblion* meaning "the book." The plural form was *ta biblia*, "the books." This is a good description of what the Bible is—a library of books.

Collectively, the Bible tells the story of God's love affair with the human race despite its sins and betrayals. Love oozes from its pages, from the first verse to the last. Genesis 1:1 says, "In the beginning God created heaven and earth." Thus, the Bible opens with a ringing affirmation of a loving Creator. God gives existence to all creatures, especially those made in God's image and likeness—human beings.

The last two verses of the Bible read: "Come, Lord Jesus. May the grace of the Lord Jesus be with you all. Amen" (Rv 22:20-21). This prayer concludes the written record of revelation by commending us to Jesus. Jesus is God's supreme gift of love, the key to our salvation and eternal life.

The various individual books of the Bible were composed over the course of approximately one thousand years. Most books of the Bible came into being through this process: *experience, reflection, oral tradition,* and *written book.* Here is some more information about each stage:

- *Experience.* God touched the daily lives of the Israelites and the early Christians in many different but consistently loving and reconciling ways. These experiences were powerful, affecting the very identity of the people. God's involvement in their lives changed them and their way of thinking.

- *Reflection.* Over time, the religious leaders and people deepened their understanding of God's presence in their midst. Prophets, for example, helped explain how God worked through events, persons, ordinary life, miracles, and the like, to instruct and guide the people.

- *Oral tradition.* The custom of people in the ancient world was to tell of God's work in their history through word of mouth. Our ancestors in the faith were storytellers whose memories were outstanding. Generation after generation would hear and then repeat the stories of God's saving action in their history. Only after time, and often during periods of crisis, would they commit anything to writing.

- *Written Book.* Eventually, the Israelites wrote down parts of their heritage. First came the Ten Commandments and parts of the Mosaic law. After the nation came into being under a king, court histories and chronicles appeared. During the Exile, scribes preserved the history of the people and wrote down the words of the prophets.

A similar process took place in the New Testament. At first, early Christians retold the Jesus story, focusing especially on the events of the passion, death, and resurrection of Jesus. Key preachers like Paul wrote letters (from around A.D. 50-64) to support the faith of their early converts and instruct them on how to live a Christian life. The early churches circulated these epistles (letters) for reading at the Sunday celebrations of the Lord's Supper.

The gospels came into being from around A.D. 65 to as late as A.D. 100. Eyewitnesses to Jesus' life were dying and distortions were setting in. Consequently, the authors of Mark, Matthew, Luke, and John composed orderly accounts of Jesus' life, his teaching, his miracles, and the saving events of his last days. These evangelists relied on the oral traditions, selecting and arranging their material to bolster the faith of the communities for whom they were writing.

One final point about the Bible: though its books offer a rich written record of God's work in human history, it is only a *partial* record. Recall the closing words of John's gospel:

> *T*here was much else that Jesus did; if it were written down in detail, I do not suppose the world itself would hold all the books that would be written (Jn 21:25).

The church holds that *sacred tradition* includes other revealed truths handed down from the apostles, truths the Bible does not spell out. One example of a revealed truth not contained in the Bible is the doctrine of the Immaculate Conception of Mary.

Check Up

Do you own a bible? Do you use it?

50

My youth minister told me to purchase a "Catholic Bible." Are the Catholic and Protestant Bibles different?

The *canon* of sacred scripture is the official list of books which the church recognizes as inspired, or "written under

the guidance and protection of the Holy Spirit." The canons
of the Catholic and Protestant bibles are slightly different.
Both Protestants and Catholics accept the same twenty-
seven New Testament books. However, Protestants gener-
ally recognize only thirty-nine Old Testament books as
inspired, while Catholics accept forty-six. The discrepancy
results from different ancient versions of the Hebrew scriptures each group draws from. Here's more explanation:

Catholics and the Septuagint. Greek was the common
spoken language in the first-century Roman Empire. The
most popular version of sacred Hebrew scriptures was a
Greek translation, known as the Septuagint. The early
church, important church Fathers, and finally the Council
of Trent (1547) accepted this translation of the Hebrew
scriptures as its Old Testament canon.

Protestants and the Jewish canon. In A.D. 90, Jewish rabbis who had survived the Roman destruction of the Temple
in A.D. 70 assembled at Jamnia, a city in northern Palestine,
to consolidate their sacred books. At this meeting, they
accepted into their official list of books only the books
which were originally written in Hebrew. They dropped
seven books from the Septuagint that were composed in
Greek in the two centuries before Christ. Those seven
books are *1 and 2 Maccabees, Judith, Tobit, Baruch, Sirach,* and
the *Wisdom of Solomon.* At the time of the Protestant Revolt,
the Reformers adopted for their canon the official list of
inspired works created by the rabbis in A.D. 90.

Most Protestant Bibles today print the disputed books
in a separate section at the back of the Bible. They refer to
these books (plus some passages in Daniel and Esther) as
apocrypha, that is, "hidden or withdrawn from common
use." Catholics recognize these books as inspired and refer
to them as *deuterocanonical,* meaning "a second canon," to
indicate that the Jews do not accept them into their official
canon.

Don't forget, however, the Bible is primarily a source of unity among Christians. Here are four points all Christians can support:

1. **Read** the Bible regularly.

2. **Pray** with the Bible.

3. **Live** the truths of the Bible in your own life.

4. **Spread** the good news of the Bible by sharing your faith.

51

Is the Bible true?

Yes, the Bible conveys God's truth. According to the Second Vatican Council, the Bible teaches "firmly, faithfully, and without error that truth which God wanted put into the sacred writings for the sake of our salvation" (*Constitution on Divine Revelation,* #11).

But if what you mean by your question is whether everything in the Bible is scientifically or historically true, the answer is "no." Think of the Bible as a library of books with many different literary forms. These include poetry, allegories, fables, speeches, fictional short stories, census lists, historical accounts, and many other types of literature. To discover the religious truth of the Bible, you must first identify what kind of literature you are reading. Then you must ask what the biblical author meant to communicate about God and salvation by using this particular literary form.

Take, for example, the parable of the Prodigal Son. Was there historically a younger son like the one Jesus described in his story, one who squandered his inheritance? Most likely, there is no real, historical person behind this passage. Jesus told this vivid short *story* to reveal in a graphic way God's forgiving love for sinners.

Similarly, in the Old Testament, it is highly doubtful that a large fish actually swallowed Jonah. Rather, this is a story that contains the powerful truth that God desires the salvation of everyone. There is, however, much historical truth in the Bible, including the chronicles of the Israelite kingdom, the gospel stories of Jesus of Nazareth, and the missionary travels of St. Paul.

It always takes prayerful reflection to understand the religious truth of the Bible. Furthermore, it is helpful to refer to a Bible commentary for further insight. Finally, Catholics can always look to the church's magisterium for help to understand the especially difficult or controversial passages.

52

Was there a "real" Adam and Eve?

A nun once asked her third-grade students, "Can any of you tell me who lived in the Garden of Eden?"

"Yes, sister," replied a little boy. "It was the Adams' family."

Certainly for this class of students, Adam and Eve were indeed real. Recall that Adam and Eve appear in the early chapters of the book of Genesis, which was written only a few centuries before the coming of Christ. Recall, also, that these chapters involve Hebrew poetry, specifically what scholars call "religious myth." This poetic writing style uses stories, parables, allegories, and the like to communicate religious truths.

Religious myth as a form of literature is *not* the same as a legend or a fairy tale. The authors of Genesis used figurative language to convey important religious truths that God wants us to know. These truths include the following:

- Human beings are created in the image and likeness of the one, true, and loving God.

- God created men and women as equals who are to care for and love each other.

- God alone creates each human soul, the spiritual principle in humans. The human soul is immortal.

- The world God made is good and for the benefit of humans.

- The misfortunes of humans, including death, result from the prideful sin and disobedience of the first man. This is what we call original sin, an essential truth of Catholic faith.

- Despite human failure, God still loved humanity. God did not abandon us. From the beginning, God had a plan to rescue humans from their sins.

Genesis is *not* a scientific treatise. It does not address the issue of whether humans descend from one set of parents or many sets of first parents. Nor does Genesis intend to tell us the historical names of our original parents. The name *Adam* means "man" or "from the earth"; Eve means "helpmate." These are symbolic names for the prototypes of humanity.

Incidentally, on the question of how many sets of parents we came from, the church has expressed a teaching. In his encyclical *Humani Generis* (1950), Pope Pius XII wrote that it is merely a theory, not a fact, that humans come from more than one set of parents (polygenesis). He taught that a belief in one set of parents (monogenesis) seems to be the only way to protect the very clear and important teaching about original sin contained in the second creation story in Genesis. The *Catechism of the Catholic Church* expresses this teaching as follows:

The account of the fall in Genesis 3 uses figurative language, but affirms a primeval event, a deed that took place *at the beginning of the history of man* (#390).

53

The book of Revelation seems impossible to understand. It's almost like a dream, what with trumpets sounding and strange beasts appearing. Also, I hear so much about the number "666" in Revelation 13:18. What does this number mean?

The book of Revelation is the last book in the Bible. It is difficult to understand because much of it is written using a highly symbolic form of writing known as *apocalypse*. Like the Old Testament book of Daniel, Revelation uses a weirdly imaginative writing style to disguise its contents should it fall into the wrong hands. At the time of its composition around A.D. 95, the Roman emperor Domitian was fiercely persecuting Christians for refusing to acknowledge the divinity of the emperor as the state religion required.

Thus, the book of Revelation is in code, with numbers and animals, for example, assigned a specific meaning. An ancient scholar commented that studying the book of

Revelation will either find us crazy or make us crazy. St. Jerome wrote that it contains more secrets than it does words.

The main purpose of the text was to strengthen the hope and determination of those suffering in the infant church. Its basic message is that God controls history and the outcome of events, not any wicked earthly rulers or forces of evil. Eventually God will usher in a golden age of justice and peace. Until that time, Christians should patiently endure suffering and live like Jesus Christ.

In Revelation 13, the author describes a vision of a beast from the sea and a beast from the earth who is also a false prophet. This prophet-monster from the land has two horns like a lamb and speaks like a dragon. It forces people to worship the first beast and kills those who do not. In verse 18, the author assigns this beast-prophet the number 666.

Bible scholars have noted that in the Hebrew and Greek languages, letters have a numerical value and that the letters QSR NRWN (Caesar Nero) in Hebrew add up to 666. Nero was the vicious persecutor of Christians in the 60s. Many believed that the evil of Nero was being equated with the person of the current emperor, Domitian.

54

I know Armageddon has something to do with the end of the world, but I'm not sure exactly what. Also, does the Bible tell us when the world is going to end or when Jesus will come again?

Armageddon is a word mentioned only once in the Bible, in Revelation 16:16. It refers to the place of the final confrontation between the forces of good and evil. In Hebrew, Armageddon means "Mountain of Megiddo," a famous battlefield of ancient Palestine.

Various sects (like the Jehovah Witnesses) have unsuccessfully tried to predict when this final battle and the end of the world will occur. The closer we are to the year 2000, people known as *millenarians* are likely to be more vocal. Millenarians interpret certain passages from the book of Revelation as stating that Christ will reign on earth for a thousand years before the world ends. For them, a symbolic number like the year 2000 signals the beginning of the end.

Be wary of groups that make scary predictions about the world's end. Some people, consciously or not, exploit the natural fear everyone has of the unknown. Their "secret" knowledge of the future gives them a type of control over others.

The church teaches that Christ will come again to judge the living and the dead (Mt 12:36). Since Jesus is a loving savior, we should not fear this day (Jn 3:17). We should, however, prepare for judgment day by serving others (Mt 24:42-44). The church does not pretend to know *when* the world will end or the nature of the events preceding it.

The church directs us to the teaching of Jesus himself. When the apostles asked him *when* the world would end, Jesus replied:

*B*ut as for that day or hour, nobody knows it
. . . no one but the Father" (Mk 13:32).

Jesus teaches that we should always be prepared for our own personal death or the end of the world by living a Christian life right now (Mk 13:33). Needless worry about the future is pointless, accomplishing nothing. Jesus instructs us to set our hearts on God's kingdom first and to trust in God's saving justice. Everything else will take care of itself (Mt

6:33-34). It is hard to improve on this formula for a happy, productive Christian life.

55

Do miracles happen today?

I believe they do, and so does my wife. To be brief, my wife and my oldest son are alive today because they survived an extremely life-threatening situation years ago during childbirth.

The attending physician, a non-Catholic, told me that it was a miracle that both survived the emergency procedure. He said he never saw anything like it in the twenty years he was chief obstetrician in a large hospital. He claimed it was God's intervention that saved them both. I fervently believe he was right, though I could never prove it to another person beyond a shadow of a doubt. But I do know that our Lord did something extraordinary to spare my wife and child.

I'm not the only one who believes that God performs miracles today. A 1989 Gallup survey revealed that 82 percent of Americans polled believed that "even today, miracles are performed by the power of God."[4]

Science supports these beliefs. For example, Catholics and others have claimed that God has performed miraculous cures of sick people—many of them terminally ill—at Lourdes, France. (This is the site of the shrine where Mary appeared to St. Bernadette Soubirous in 1858.) Between 1948 and 1993, more than thirteen hundred people claimed that God cured them at Lourdes. It is impossible to "prove" that all of these were miracles. But an objective commission of scientists and medical personnel, using the most stringent criteria, has led church authorities to conclude that at least eighteen of these cures were indeed miracles.[5]

In addition, church history is full of examples of God's miraculous intervention in the lives of people. This is true even in our own day. For example, it is possible to view the incorrupt bodies of some saints (these bodies were not mummified at death). Science cannot explain this phenomena. At Fatima, Portugal, where Mary appeared in 1917, more than seventy thousand people were present on October 13 when the sun appeared to plummet out of the sky. A priest of this century, Padre Pio, bore the stigmata (the wounds of Christ) and cured many people during his lifetime. For example, he cured a lady of blindness. She has no pupils, yet she is able to see.

Many miracles are associated with the saints. In his acclaimed book *Making Saints*,[6] Kenneth L. Woodward describes the exhaustive, "very severe," and carefully thought-out procedure the Vatican uses to determine if a candidate for canonization has worked a miracle. A doctor, whose job it is to determine if these medical wonders attributed to saints are really miracles, calls them "fantastic, incredible, and well-documented." Science fiction does not compare to the works God sometimes accomplishes through his friends, those holy people we call saints.

Like a wise mother, however, the church is not gullible. Church authorities always try to find a natural explanation for marvelous events brought to their attention. A recent example has been the church's reluctance to state that any supernatural events have taken place at Medjugorje in the former Yugoslavia. But after careful and exhaustive examination, there are times when the church is willing to state that God has intervened miraculously in our world. Why? Because miracles do happen.

What's a Miracle?

Biblical scholar Fr. John P. Meier provides an up-to-date, comprehensive definition of miracle:

✛ It is an unusual, startling, extraordinary and observable event.

✛ Human abilities or known forces that operate in space and time cannot explain this event.

✛ It results from a special act of God, doing what no human person can do.[7]

56

Does Satan really exist?

The word *Satan* means "adversary." Both the scripture and church teaching hold that Satan, also known as the devil, does indeed exist.

Satan, along with other demons, was at first a good angel, made by a loving God. (Angels are spiritual beings with free will, naturally superior to humans; angels were created by God before the world began.) But scripture reveals that these "bad angels" freely sinned against God (2 Pt 2:4). They radically and irrevocably rejected God and God's reign. A hint of their sin appears in Genesis when the "father of lies" told our first parents, "You will be like God" (Gn 3:5). By trying to make themselves God, the bad angels rebelled against a loving, gracious Creator. Filled with hate and unwilling to repent, Satan and those other devils were driven from God's presence.

The sin of Satan and the devils turned them into vengeful, hateful, bitter creatures who oppose God and God's plan for humanity. The gospels present Satan as Jesus' prime enemy who was constantly trying to turn Jesus away from his divine mission. Jesus spoke often of Satan, calling him a "murderer from the beginning." But Jesus came to defeat Satan, saying that he saw him fall from the sky like lightning. Jesus' many exorcisms previewed Satan's downfall.

Jesus' passion, death, resurrection, and ascension definitively overpowered the forces of evil and the demons. These saving events reversed the effects of the disobedience of our first parents. Through the Paschal Mystery, Jesus Christ conquered sin, death, diabolical power, and our alienation from God.

It is a mystery to us why God permits the devil to tempt us and to work against God's kingdom. But our faith reassures us that God's reign is growing. The Risen Lord, through the Holy Spirit, is in charge of human history, gently guiding it until that day of his Second Coming. On that day, everyone will recognize the sovereign divinity of Jesus Christ.

Satan does indeed exist. But if you stay close to Jesus you need never fear his work.

57

What is "demon possession"? Does it happen today?

Much of what previous centuries termed "demon possession" was probably symptoms of psychological disorders or incidents of seizures. Having said that, the church does hold that demonic possession is possible, though extremely rare. Demon possession includes phenomena like speaking in unknown languages, exhibiting "superhuman" strength, and revealing hidden secrets. A possessed person may also engage in other offensive behavior like uttering blasphemies.

When long medical treatments do not cure the symptoms of an apparently possessed person, a bishop may permit a mature priest to perform the church's rite *of exorcism*. Historically, this rite has shown that the devil is no match for Jesus Christ.

Because it is extremely rare, you should not expect to encounter this type of observable, physical activity of the devil. You should, however, stay close to Jesus in prayer. Strive to live a Christian life with the help of the eucharist and the sacrament of penance. Avoid fascination with the occult or demons or superstitious practices. Satan, "the father of lies," uses these ungodly, dark realities to woo a person away from Christ, the true Light and Life.

58

Why do we have to die?

Death is all around us. Government statistics report that 2,268,000 Americans died in 1993. This averages to more than one death per second! These facts make death seem very natural, and it is.

Though our nature is mortal, death—the separation of the soul from the body—was not in God's plan for us. Death entered the world because of sin, the original sin of the first man. Humans would have been immune from death had not Adam proudly disobeyed God and put his will first. Death is the result of Adam's sin. Death is our enemy. The Book of Job calls it "the king of terrors."

But our Christian faith helps us to face death. Jesus himself transformed the meaning of death. In fact, in the Incarnation Jesus freely accepted death as part of the human condition. Like any normal person who would face a painful death, Jesus anguished over it. But he accepted death in obedience to his Father's will. And because of this act of obedience, God raised Jesus up. Jesus' resurrection has defeated sin and death, once and for all.

Every person who has ever lived walked a road that ended in the grave. Fame, personal wealth, power, influence, prestige, earthly success can never take us beyond the valley of death. Only Jesus can do that. As St. Paul proclaimed:

> Just as all die in Adam, so in Christ all will be brought to life. . . . The last of the enemies to be done away with is death (1 Cor 15:22, 26).

Faith and trust in Jesus Christ and living in conformity with his Father's will put us on the right road. Death then becomes, in the words of St. Bernard of Clairvaux, "the gate of life."

"I Need Jesus Now"

Once a missionary preached to an old Indian chief about Jesus Christ, describing Jesus as God's only way to heaven. "The Jesus' road sounds like a good road," the chief observed. "But I have always followed the Indian road, and I don't want to change now."

A year later, the chief was dying of a fatal disease. He called the missionary to his side and asked for baptism. "I need Jesus now," the dying chief said. "The Indian road stops here. It cannot take me through the valley."

59

What is reincarnation? What does the church teach about reincarnation?

Reincarnation is a belief, primarily held by Hinduism, that a person's soul after death is reborn into another body. According to Hindu belief, this happens as often as it takes a person's soul (Atman) to reach purification from worldliness. When one achieves perfection, the Atman will be free of the body and enter a state of bliss known as Nirvana. In Nirvana, the individual soul loses itself in the Brahman, the hidden and impersonal essence of the universe.

But if a soul does not attain purification and enlightenment (due to sin, materialism, sensuality, false beliefs about the true self), it will rejoin a body that matches its character. Thus, there is a connection between one's actions in this life and the type of body one will get in the new life. This law of Karma, in its unrefined form, holds that a particularly evil individual might come back as a lower life form. Reincarnation is directly opposed to Christian revelation. The church does not accept belief in reincarnation for the following reasons:

1. Scripture reveals that we die only once and then meet God in judgment. This judgment decides our fate for eternity (Hb 9:7). Many other biblical teachings reject reincarnation. (See, for example, Ps 49:19, Lk 16:19-31, 20:36, and 2 Cor 5:8.)

2. Reincarnation comes from a philosophy that holds that material creation is either evil or unreal. Christians, on the other hand, believe

that all of God's created reality, including our bodies and the world itself, is both real and very good. Though in need of Christ's redemption, the human body is a great, good gift from God.

3. Reincarnation denies the basic truth of our faith, "the resurrection of the body." Jesus' appearances to his disciples in recognizable form after his resurrection hints at our own resurrection when our souls will reunite with our transformed and glorified bodies.

4. In some way, reincarnation follows the motto "If you don't succeed, try, try, again." Reincarnation holds that a soul will eventually save itself by finally "getting it right" through purification and enlightenment. Christianity teaches that salvation comes from Jesus alone: "Only in him [Jesus] is there salvation" (Acts 4:12). Salvation is God's pure gift for us, something we cannot earn.

60

What will heaven and hell be like?

Our Christian faith holds the existence of both a heaven and hell. What each is "like" one can only speculate based on what we know about God through the teachings of Jesus. C. S. Lewis compared heaven and hell as follows:

In hell they talk a lot about love. In heaven they just do it.

Hell is an unending church service without God. Heaven is God without a church service.

In hell, everything is pornographic and no one is excited. In heaven everything is exciting and there is no pornography.

In hell there is sex without pleasure. In heaven there is pleasure without sex.

Hell is a bad dream from which you never wake. Heaven is waking from which you never need to sleep.

We cannot begin to imagine the joy in store for us in heaven. As St. Paul wrote:

What no eye has seen and no ear has heard, what the mind of man cannot visualize; all that God has prepared for those who love him (1 Cor 2:9).

In heaven we will be:
  ~forever in the presence of a God who is love,
    joy, peace
  ~happy and fulfilled to the utmost
  ~able to know God as God really is
  ~present with God and all God's other beloved
    friends, including our own family members
    and friends.

Heaven is often described like a shining, crystal city or an incredibly delightful, joy-filled banquet. But these images pale in comparison to the reality. Imagine describing a beautiful sunset to a blind person or the kiss of a loved one to a person who cannot feel. You can only hint at the reality, just like heaven.

Oppositely, hell is eternal separation from God. Jesus himself referred to hell often in his own instructions to his contemporaries (for example, Mk 9:43-48 and Mt 25:46). The New Testament also reveals that hell is a place of consciousness and pain (Lk 16:23-24,28) and a place of darkness (Mt 8:12). Hell involves eternal separation from loved ones (Lk 13:28), with no hope of release (Mt 25:46, Hb 6:2). It also involves the torment of memory (Lk 16:27-28).

God does not send us to hell; God wills the salvation of everyone. Yet God respects a person's free, stubborn decision to say "no" to the gift of salvation. If one dies in the state of alienation from God (mortal sin), then the punishment is hell.

Though writers often use fire to describe hell, the church reminds us that this is only an image. Christ reveals that hell is eternal separation from God, the worst fate that could befall us. And though we believe there is such a place, the church has never defined how many people are actually in hell.

We were made to be with God in heaven—forever. We should resolve to live faith-filled, loving, Christ-like lives to get there. As the famous French writer Victor Hugo wrote, "Good actions are the invisible hinges of the doors of heaven."

My girlfriend dropped me. Now she's dating someone else. What can I do to get over her?

Is there such a thing as the ideal person to date?
What should I be looking for in a date?

I'm c_____
"not d_____
movie_____
tell m_____

What_____
church_____
lives?_____

I thi_____
What_____

How f_____

Is hor_____

I thi_____
anyon_____

Why_____
ing to_____
before_____

How _____
sex?_____

Is date rape a crime? How can I protect myself
from date rape?

AIDS seems so out of control. I'm worried about
becoming infected. Should I be? What does the
church teach about AIDS?

Chapter

4

Let's Talk Some More About Sex

What the Church Really Says About Love, Dating, and Sexuality

A father was dreading the mandatory talk with his son about *it*. Finally, he mustered up the courage to broach the topic with his young teen.

"Well, son," he said, "let's talk about sex." The youth replied, "Sure, dad, what do you want to know?"

This chapter discusses some questions teens ask and some of the topics they often assume to know quite a bit about. Perhaps you may think you know *all* about dating, relationships, and sex.

The church and parents often get a bum rap and are portrayed as heavy-handed in these areas. Read along. You may find that church teaching is very truthful in these challenging areas of human life and can be of help to you.

61

My girlfriend dropped me. Now she's dating someone else. What can I do to get over her?

Breaking up with someone will naturally bring hurt. There's no doubt that your pain is real. You may have expressed your love verbally, shared your deepest thoughts and feelings and dreams, and exchanged various signs of affection. You took a risk in getting close to her, and now you may feel as if you were betrayed. You may also feel a sense of loss and be confused as to why your relationship ended. These painful feelings are often expressed in:

◆ disordered thinking and attention (for example, you can't concentrate at school)

◆ undesirable behavior (for example, you listen to sad music)

◆ persistent negative emotions (depression, anxiety, and anger)

◆ physical complaints (for example, a poor appetite)

What can help you get over a broken relationship? Try the following:

1. *Break contact.* Accept the fact that the relationship is

over and let go of any false hope of "getting back together." Avoid calling the person or running into her at school. And don't keep tabs on her through a friend.

2. *Keep busy.* Develop new interests. Meet new people. Go out with your friends, especially in mixed groups of girls and guys. The old adage "there are plenty of fish in the sea" really does apply. You will begin dating again. But slow down. It's usually not a good idea to jump into a new relationship right away. Give yourself some time to get your emotions in order again.

3. *Stop blaming yourself.* If it was not your fault that the friendship broke up, why get down on yourself? If it was your fault, then learn from the experience. Remember, "the only mistake is not to learn from our mistakes." It could also be no one is to blame for the breakup. Your relationship was simply not meant to be.

4. *Trust the Lord.* Ask for God's help in getting over the hurt and learning from the experience. God will help you focus on your good and loving attributes and will help you to get through this time. The Lord's love heals all.

62

Is there such a thing as the ideal person to date? What should I be looking for in a date?

Let's face it. Many of today's young women like the following when they go looking for guys: good looks, athletic prowess, and popularity. Some even go after guys with fancy cars. And guys? They hunt for good-looking, popular, fun-loving girls who make them feel important.

No one can deny that these qualities, some superficial, initially cause sparks to fly between teens. However, it's best to date people who you like first as true friends. That means sharing the same interests, being of compatible personalities, holding the same important beliefs and values.

Also note that trust, respect, and care form the basis for any healthy relationship. No one person is really ideal, but there are several ideal traits. Be on the lookout for the following. Ask yourself, is this person:

- considerate? (Does the person ever ask about *you* and *your* interests?)

- honest? (Does the person look you in the eye and tell you the truth?)

- loyal? (Will this person stand by your side in times of trouble?)

- intelligent? (Does the person have a lively, creative mind that helps you stretch your own?)

- kind? (Is the person thoughtful and loving?)

- dependable? (Does the person follow through on his or her commitments?)

- interesting? (Is this person fun to talk to? Does he or she have a variety of interests?)

- affectionate? (Can this person accept and give compliments? Does he or she smile and laugh? Is the person warm and approachable?)

Find a person with a good number of these qualities, and you have likely found a winner!

What Do You Say?

- Design your own list of desirable traits for the ideal date. How many traits on your list are physical traits? intellectual traits? personality traits? spiritual traits?

- Discuss qualities that the media push as most desirable in a male or female teen. For example, analyze the articles in some magazines targeted for teens. Are the media selling an impossible, unrealistic, or superficial ideal? Explain.

63

What's the difference between love and infatuation?

Infatuation is usually based on a strong physical or sexual attraction. When you instantly fall in love with someone you hardly know, you are probably infatuated. This "love at first sight" blinding "hot" attraction to someone is emotional rather than rational. You cannot build a lasting relationship on infatuation. As a wise person once said, "To marry a woman for her beauty is like buying a home for its paint."

Because it is superficial, instantaneous, and emotionally charged, infatuation won't last. It is, however, possible for infatuation to evolve into true romantic love where the feelings of the other person are more important than your own. But you need time to get to know and care for the other person. True love, in contrast with infatuation, is mature, stable, and rooted in reality.

So what to do if you are infatuated with another from time to time? "Puppy love," as infatuation is often called, certainly doesn't make the world go around, but it can make the trip worthwhile as long as it is understood for what it is.

Also, be sure to help the other person understand infatuation just in case your beauty and charm are blinding him or her. Deepen your "mutual admiration society" by getting to know each other as you *really* are. Do not let the feeling of infatuation lead you to disrespect yourself or the other person, especially in the area of sexuality.

What's the Difference Between Love and Infatuation?

The Myth of Infatuation	The Reality of Love
Fall in to and out of quickly; fickle	Grows slowly with time; faithful
Based on superficial knowledge of a person	Rooted in a deepening knowledge of the other
Is fleeting	Is lasting
Lives in a dream world, always expecting the other to help create a perfect world	Is realistic, practical, accepting the other's imperfections and limitations
Emotional roller coaster	Stable and consistent, building self-confidence
Driven by suspicion and jealousy; possessive	Allows the other person freedom to develop; mutually supportive

Wants immediate gratification	Is patient and respect-ful of the other
Impressed with externals: looks, status, money	Unconditional accep-tance of another
In love with the idea of love	In love with a person
Takes	Gives
Self-centered	Other-directed
Can be fake to get the other to accept	Always honest

Immature love says:"I love you because I need you."

Mature love says:"I need you because I love you."

~Erich Fromm, psychologist

64

I'm confused about sex. All the warnings about "not doing it" make it seem that sex is bad. Yet, movies, advertisements, and even my own feelings tell me it's good. What's the truth?

With all the news of AIDS and other sexually transmitted diseases, teen pregnancies, adultery, divorce, abortion, pornography, child molestation, rape, crimes of passion, and a host of other headline-grabbing tragedies, it is easy to get the impression that sex is bad.

But sex isn't bad. What can be bad is what some people do with their sexuality. They distort and misuse it for selfish motives. For example, some treat others as objects for pleasure. In the process, they disfigure their own personal dignity and hurt another person.

Please keep in mind that neither Hollywood, nor *Penthouse*, nor advertisers, nor the latest rock star invented sex. God did! God made us sexual beings, male and female, and implanted in us a strong "urge to merge" for two basic reasons: First, sexual intercourse enables a man and woman who have pledged a lifetime commitment to one another in marriage to show their love for another in an exciting, fun way. Second, sex empowers men and women to share in God's work of bringing forth new life. For these two reasons, sex is good, very good!

You should thank God for this great gift of sex. But you should remember the lesson you have likely heard often: Sexual intercourse is a gift designed for married couples only. Think of it this way: Sex is a lot like fire. In a fireplace it is warm and cozy. On a stove, it cooks the food we need for physical sustenance. But outside the hearth or oven, it is destructive and wild, capable of causing great damage.

The trick is to keep the fire of sexual desire so present in your teen years contained so it doesn't get out of control. You'll have strong urges, but you don't *have* to act on them. Remember, no one ever died from lack of sex. Also, try to make these four practices part of your game plan to live an upright life in the area of sex:

◆ Keep in touch with Jesus through prayer. He will always support your efforts to keep the fire in the hearth.

◆ Associate with wholesome friends who share your values.

◆ Receive Jesus in the eucharist.

◆ If you do fail in the area of sex, be sure to ask for God's forgiveness in the sacrament of reconciliation. Remember that Jesus came to help sinners (see Lk 5:30-32). The sacrament of penance is a powerful help he left for your benefit.

Finally, don't lose your perspective about sex. It is not the be-all and end-all of your life. What's most important is what kind of loving person you are. If you grow at being more loving toward God, other people, and yourself, you will find that your strong sexual feelings will be directed into positive energy that can assist you in becoming the person God calls you to be.

65

What does sex have to do with religion? Why is the church always getting involved with people's sex lives?

The church teaches in areas of sexual morality because the misuse of sex hurts people and causes unhappiness. Jesus cared about the happiness of people and their well-being, in this life and in the next. As his representative and

presence in the world, the church—often called a wise
mother—has seen the damage people suffer when they distort God's will. It has a Christ-given duty to call people to
faithful observance of God's laws, including laws in the
area of sexuality.

Like any good and loving mother, the church speaks
out on behalf of our interests in many different areas,
including:

- **Emotionally**. Sex outside of marriage almost
  always results in emotional pain. Premarital or
  extramarital sex is usually associated with feelings like guilt, regret, and anxiety. Self-esteem
  always suffers.

- **Physically.** There are more than fifty sexually
  transmitted diseases that cause many physical
  problems or even death. Over one million
  teenage girls get pregnant every year. Many of
  these pregnancies result in abortion. (There are
  1.6 million abortions in the United States annually.)

- **Spiritually.** Sex is meant to involve one's whole
  being—body, mind, and spirit. St. Paul tells us
  that when we misuse sex, we hurt our relationships with God and others. For example, how
  would a future marriage partner feel knowing
  you had sex with several other people? Would
  he or she ever be able to trust you? Would you
  ever be able to trust yourself?

When we use our sexuality as God intends, it can
enhance our happiness. When we misuse it, it can tear us
apart and bring us misery. Why does the church get
involved with sexual issues? Primarily to remind us—
against the propaganda of the day—that following God's
way is the true path to happiness.

66

—

I think about sex quite often. Is that wrong? What is meant by "impure thoughts?"

Sexual thoughts, like sexual desire and passion, are natural and normal. It is difficult for any healthy person *not* to have these thoughts. This is especially true of teenagers whose bodies are raging with hormones and who are discovering the beauties and the mysteries of members of the opposite sex. And it is doubly true in a society that bombards us constantly in movies, television, and advertisements with suggestive sexual imagery, much of it very explicit.

The phrase "impure thoughts" usually refers to *lust*, "the inordinate desire for sexual pleasure." The vice of lust makes a god out of sex. Lust is a vice that deliberately inflames one's sexual desires for someone, going beyond the boundaries God has set for healthy and moral sexual attraction. It leads people to look at others as objects for their own sexual pleasure. Jesus condemned lust when he said that "everyone who looks at another with lust" is guilty of adultery (Mt 5:28).

How can you differentiate between normal sexual thoughts and desires and lust? Consider the following:

Say a good-looking person walks by. He or she attracts your eye. You have warm feelings for this person. You find this person desirable. These are natural and normal feelings. Neither your thoughts nor feelings are lustful.

Lust, however, enters the picture when you *deliberately* entertain impure thoughts about this person. You continue to fantasize sexually with the sole purpose of inflaming your passions. For example, you begin to imagine what he or she would look like undressed. Or you try to picture what the person would be like as a bed partner. You stay with these thoughts, take delight in them, allow them "to turn you on." Sometimes, you might even allow them to lead you to masturbate.

Lust, like any vice, is wrong and sinful. It is a sin of weakness. However, lust is not the worst sin in the world. Pride, arrogance, greed, prejudice, and hate are worse sins because they transform us into uncaring and unloving people.

If you are struggling with impure thoughts, you are in good company. Even a great saint like St. Augustine of Hippo fought a lifelong battle to gain mastery of his passions.

To counteract impure thoughts, think wholesome thoughts when tempted to dwell on sexual fantasies. A vice is a bad habit; a virtue is a good habit. Develop good habits by thinking about good and productive things.

Also, turn to Jesus and the Blessed Mother for their help in times of temptation. And if you slip, don't get down on yourself. Remember that Jesus left us the sacrament of reconciliation to provide forgiveness and encouragement. And the Lord gave us his very self in the eucharist to give us strength to live the right way.

67

Is masturbation wrong?

By definition, *masturbation* is the deliberate stimulation of the genital organs to get solitary sexual pleasure.

Note that a person who masturbates is concerned only with his or her needs; that is, seeking pleasure for its own sake. This behavior is wrong because God meant sexual activity to be *relational*. God gave us human beings sex organs—and the pleasure associated with them—to share with a member of the opposite sex to whom we have totally committed our lives. God intended that we use our sexual faculties to communicate our deep, unconditional love for our marriage partner and to cooperate with that person and God in procreating human life.

Many people masturbate to escape problems. But note the word *escape*. Masturbation does not cure one's problems, and it quickly becomes habit-forming. After masturbating, people usually feel spiritually empty and psychologically depressed. They still have problems and their self-esteem is usually worse than it was before.

Another down side to this habit is that one who masturbates quickly gets used to immediate self-gratification. When dating starts, the habit of immediate gratification can easily translate into using another merely as an object for personal pleasure. True love for another demands discipline and control, patience, and the ability to say "no."

Do people sin mortally when they masturbate? Recall that masturbation thwarts both aims of God's design for sexual activity: the sharing of love and the giving of life. Because love and life are serious issues, masturbation is something that in itself is "an intrinsically and gravely disordered action" (CCC, #2352). This means that if a person knowingly and freely chooses to masturbate contrary to God's law, then the conditions are present for mortal sin.

But the church wisely teaches that certain factors can *lessen* or even erase one's guilt or moral blameworthiness in the case of masturbation. These include immaturity, anxiety, the force of an acquired habit, and other social or psychological factors (like compulsion).

If you have acquired the habit of masturbation, don't get discouraged. God still loves you. Ask yourself if you are honestly trying to avoid those situations that cause you to fail in sexual self-control. For example:

—Do you avoid pornography?

—Do you make an honest effort to live an upright and loving life, caring for others?

—Do you try to gain self-control, for example, by asking for our Lord's help in prayer and in the sacraments of confession and holy communion?

A "yes" response to these questions is a good sign that your acts of masturbation may not be completely deliberate.

A final word of advice: Remember that every adult known to you is struggling to live a chaste life. They were young once, too, and they remember very well the storms of the teen years. Today's world is sex-saturated. It scoffs at Christ's command to reserve sexual activity for marriage. Everyone needs help to live as Christ intends us to live as his disciples. Please, don't be afraid to approach a priest-friend, a trusted teacher, or another adult you love to discuss your struggles in this area. He or she will understand. And this person will profoundly respect you for asking for his or her advice and help.

68

How far can I go sexually?

Teens (and adults) have been asking this question from time immemorial. What they usually mean is, "How much pleasure can I get from playing with another's body (and he or she playing with mine) before I break God's law?" When this is what is meant, then the person is only concerned with using the other person as an object for his or her own gratification.

This, of course, is wrong. Sex is not a plaything. Using another person for one's own sexual pleasure violates that person's dignity. Sex is the language of love between totally committed persons. Sexual intimacy without the true love commitment found only in marriage leads to rejection. In our day, we have also seen how it often results in the tragic abortions of children conceived outside of the marriage bond.

Sex is beautiful, exciting, passionate, and progressive. Once the sexual passion gets started, its natural outcome is greater intimacy and eventual union with another. God intends this union, of course, for a husband and a wife in the sacrament of marriage. The term for premarital sexual intercourse is *fornication;* the term for extramarital sex is *adultery.* In many places in scripture, any form of fornication or adultery is condemned (see: Dt 5:21, Mt 5:27-30, Hb 13:4, 1 Thes 4:3-5, and 1 Cor 6:9, 18).

Premarital sex is like the TV commercial about a certain brand of potato chips. The advertisement says, "You can't have just one." Once a person has entered the danger zone of premarital sex, it is difficult indeed to draw back. "Drawing lines," however, can indeed help you avoid the sin of fornication.

The following behaviors are "over the line" on the negative and destructive side and should be avoided:

1. Prolonged kissing which leads to open-mouthed kissing, including the last stages of "necking," nibbling on the ears and the neck.

2. Any type of *petting.* Petting is intimate touching (sexual foreplay) of another's "private parts." It arouses the passions and leads to sexual intercourse. Light petting includes the touching of cov-

ered or bared breasts. Heavy petting includes the touching of genitals, either covered or bared. It also includes oral sex and genital-to-genital contact.

3. Sexual intercourse. Prolonged kissing and petting lead naturally to this behavior which is fraught with many physical, emotional, and spiritual dangers for unmarried teens.

A guideline that can answer your question and keep you on the positive side of the safety zone is: *Before marriage, limit yourself to hand-holding, hugs, and light kissing as ways to show affection.*

Positive Guidelines for Handling Sexually Tempting Situations

- Kiss only with the lips closed.

- Don't touch another's "private parts." Beware of roaming hands. Don't allow someone to touch your private parts.

- Keep your clothes on.

- Stop immediately when genital feelings are aroused.

- Stop immediately when you feel yourself losing control.

69

Is homosexuality a sin?

Catholic teaching on sexual morality has its roots in the first chapter of the first book of the Bible. According to Genesis 1:27-28:

Male and female he created them.
God blessed them, saying to them, "Be fruitful,
multiply, fill the earth and subdue it."

This passage is fundamental. It tells us that God made man and woman to be *complementary* persons. God endowed humans with a sexual nature to help God in the task of creating new human life. According to God's plan, therefore, sexual sharing should take place only in marriage. In that bond, a man and woman unite as one. They share their unconditional love, remaining open to any new life God may send to them.

The church teaches that it is sinful and morally wrong to engage in sexual practices outside of marriage. This includes sexual activity between persons of the same gender, activity that is not complementary and not procreative. St. Paul condemns homosexual practices as "against nature" (Rm 1:27).

Homosexual genital *acts* are sinful because they misuse the sexual faculty as God intended it. Like heterosexual premarital and extramarital sexual activity, homosexual acts deny the life-giving and unitive nature of sexual love that can take place only in a marriage between a man and a woman. If a person engages in premarital, extramarital, or homosexual acts with knowledge and freedom, then he or she is guilty of serious sin.

However, please note carefully the following. The church draws a distinction between homosexual *activity*, which is always wrong, and a homosexual *orientation*. A true homosexual orientation is an enduring sexual attraction to persons of the same sex. This typically results in a desire to engage in genital, sexual activity with members of the same sex.

A true homosexual orientation is *not* sinful because a person does not choose to have these desires. (Similarly, a person is not "guilty" of being tall or short.) To date, science has not discovered the precise cause of a homosexual orientation. Is it genetic, hormonal, learned or induced through sexual experience, family rearing, or a combination of one or more factors? No one knows for sure. But a homosexual orientation is not sinful because a person does not deliberately choose it.

Our culture, tragically, often fails to distinguish between a homosexual orientation and homosexual acts. As a result, society often stigmatizes homosexuals as sex fiends who cannot or refuse to control their sexual behavior. These judgments about all homosexuals are cruel and unjust. People are not morally blameworthy for having a homosexual orientation. It is prejudice of the worst kind to lump everyone together, claiming that all homosexuals do evil things and are therefore condemnable.

Jesus expects us to treat every human person with dignity and respect. This includes everyone, regardless of sexual orientation. To hate, display violence toward, or reject anyone is un-Christian, and likely sinful itself.

70

—

I think I may be gay, and I am scared to tell anyone how I feel. What should I do?

The first thing you should be aware of is that it is very likely you are not gay. In recent years the media have stated as fact that approximately 10 percent of the population is homosexual. Recent reliable studies, however, have shown that perhaps only one percent of the population has an exclusively homosexual orientation. That means that statistically it is unlikely you are gay.

You might examine why you think you might be. Because of inexperience, some teens mistakenly conclude that they have a homosexual orientation because of one of the following characteristics or experiences. But *none* of these means you are homosexual.

- *Previous engagement in sexual activity with someone of the same sex.* A one-time experience, whether experimental or a form of sexual abuse, does not determine your sexual orientation.

- *Awkwardness around members of the opposite sex.* Even if it seems that all your peers have it more together than you do, know that most people feel uneasy in the presence of members of the opposite sex. It takes some people years to get over their shyness. Be patient with yourself. Many people don't start dating until the college years and even later.

- *Strong, same-sex friendships with powerful feelings of affection.* This is normal and healthy for human growth and development.

- *A certain personality type.* It is perfectly normal if a guy is quiet, shy, gentle, and sensitive. It is OK if a girl is aggressive, rough-and-tumble, and athletic. Having these types of personalities does not mean a person is homosexual.

- *Someone of the same sex has made a "pass" at you.* This simply means you are an attractive person. Be grateful. It does not mean *you* are gay.

What should you do? Your best bet at this point *is* to talk your fears over with someone you trust—a parent, a priest, or a counselor. It is perfectly normal for teens—as they mature—to experience confusion about their sexuality. What you need is someone to tell you that you are lovable for who you are as a human being. Sexuality is only a part of who you are; it is not the total picture. This is why it is wrong for a person to identify so strongly with his or her sexual orientation. A person should never forget that he or she is first a lovable child of God, a brother or sister to all others. If it turns out you do have a true homosexual orientation, that is the way you have been made. There is nothing sinful about this orientation (see Question 69). God and the church offer much support to homosexuals to live the chaste lifestyle to which they are called.

Finally, please remember to be compassionate toward all those who are suffering with sexual-identity questions. We should recall Jesus' warning to the bystanders who wanted to kill the woman caught in adultery: "Let the one among you who is guiltless be the first to throw a stone at her" (Jn 8:7).

71
—

Why is the church so against a guy and a girl living together before marriage? Living together before marriage may help to lower the divorce rate.

Some people "live together" as a type of trial marriage. They often claim they are doing this to see if they are sexually and emotionally "compatible" for the serious relationship of marriage.

In truth, living together is just another form of *premarital sex*. A couple is engaging in the total intimacy of sexual intercourse without having made the unconditional commitment of marriage. The quality and degree of the commitment fall far short of the public, permanent promise of marriage. (Incidentally, research data shows that people who live together are *more* likely to get divorced after marriage. Furthermore, around 80 percent of those who cohabit break up—often with emotional scars.)

To understand more of the church's reasoning, think of sexual intercourse as a form of communication that conveys profound meaning. As body-language, sex says: "I am giving you my entire self, completely and exclusively. This act is a declaration of our total commitment to each other." For this action to be moral, that is, in harmony with God's plan, it should take place only when the reality of the entire relationship is one of total self-giving. This reality takes place only in marriage, where a couple has openly promised to love each other "for better or for worse, in sickness and in health" as long as they both shall live.

To engage in sexual intercourse outside of marriage— even out of motives of love—is to misuse this profound and beautiful symbol of communication. In reality, people are being dishonest when they engage in premarital sex. They are not being true to themselves. Sexual love-making should speak the language of full commitment. But actually the man and woman who are not married can always bail out. People always get hurt when they misuse God's gifts. And this can happen even with couples who say they love one another.

True love speaks the language of forever. The church promotes saving sex until marriage because sexual intercourse is both the symbol and expression of the permanent commitment of true love. Premarital *love* is the best preparation for marriage. Note how St. Paul lists *patience* as the first quality of love in 1 Corinthians 13. If you really love someone, you will wait for marriage before having sex.

72

How do I resist someone who is pressuring me for sex?

The old saying goes, "An ounce of prevention is worth a pound of cure." The best way to thwart any pressure for sex from a date is to prepare yourself ahead of time. Consider the following game plan:

1. *Know your standards.* Even before you go out on a date, say "no" in your mind and heart to any activity beyond hand-holding, hugs, and light kisses. (See Question 68.) Draw the line ahead of time and never cross it.

2. *Dress modestly.* Some girls love to tease guys to distraction, but in their minds they never intend for the guys to get to "first base." Many guys think with their groins, not their brains. If one person is sending out nonverbal, "seduce-me" messages, the partner will often interpret them as "anything goes." So, girls, stay away from tight, low-cut, clothes that are known to turn guys on. And guys, dress and speak modestly yourselves, and only date girls who respect themselves as persons, not objects for lust.

3. *Avoid sexually suggestive movies and conversation.* Stay away from sexually explicit films that are likely to enflame your passions and heighten your lust. Do not

talk about sexually suggestive topics, especially concerning your own relationship. Improper talk does lead to improper actions.

4. *Stay away from alcohol and drugs.* Nothing lowers the resolve to be chaste more than alcohol and other drugs. They lessen the ability to think clearly, to know right from wrong. Alcohol and drug abuse are the slippery slope to promiscuity. Make a contract with yourself and your date *not* to drink or do drugs.

5. *Plan the specifics of your date ahead of time.* When you have "nothing to do," you may end up getting sexually involved. Always have some back-up plans in case your main plans fall through.

6. *Avoid parking in "make-out" locales.* Besides the obvious temptations, you are also likely prey to criminals and to scrutiny by the police at such places.

7. *Say "no" strongly and firmly if your date begins to pressure you.* Guys especially have learned to push the right buttons to get what they want. Remember, you do not have to explain your "no" to your partner. If your date persists, ask him to take you home. If he refuses, leave him and call a parent or a friend to come to pick you up. You might be a bit embarrassed. But that's a small price to pay to maintain your values.

Saying No with Feeling

Here are three lines people use to pressure another into having sex and some possible responses. Devise some clever ways to say "no" to the lines that follow.

◆ "I love you. Don't you love me?"

   R: "Yes, I do. And that's why I am saying 'no.' And if you *really* love me, you'll respect my wishes."

◆ "Everyone is doing it."

   R: "That's not so because *I'm* not!"

◆ "It's not that big a deal."

   R: "It is to me. I'm saving sex for my future spouse. That's how God wants it. That's how I want it."

◆ "I heard you're uptight about sex. Prove it isn't so."

   R:

◆ "Who are you saving it for?"

   R:

◆ "Is there something the matter with me?"

   R:

◆ "We don't have to go all the way."

   R:

73

Is date rape a crime? How can I protect myself from date rape?

Rape is sexual intercourse or oral sex forced on you against your will. *Date rape* takes place whenever someone forces you to have intercourse or oral sex against your wishes while on a date. One out of four women report that a date has tried to rape them, despite their vehement protests. Almost seventy-five percent of rapes take place between people who know each other. The "force" involved includes physical harm, the threat of physical harm, or intimidating threats like, "If you don't have sex, get out of the car now and walk home!"

No one *ever* owes another person any form of romantic affection. For example, you don't owe sexual favors to someone just because the person paid for the date. Tell your date if and when you feel pressured. Don't be timid. If the person refuses to listen or argues with you, the person obviously does *not* love, care, or respect you.

Rape is a violent crime and against the law whether it occurs on a date or not. Always report it! If possible, tell your parents or another adult you trust. They will give you the support you need to stop the rapist, who will do it again if left unchecked.

No one "deserves" the dehumanization of rape or other sexual abuse.

Similarly, do not put up with verbal abuse on a date. Rude and obscene remarks as well as cruel put-downs are abusive. You do not have to take this kind of treatment. If your date is not treating you with respect, leave immediately *before* you get hurt.

When it comes to avoiding date rape, remember that a peck of common sense is worth a bushel of first-hand experience. Follow these guidelines:

- ◆ Date only people you know. Your best bet is to date someone who is already a friend. Blind dates are always risky.

- ◆ At the beginning of your relationship, date only in group settings. Rapists want isolation to pull off their crime.

- ◆ Avoid "parking" in the car for the purpose of "making out." Especially stay away from isolated areas. You are inviting trouble otherwise.

◆ Stay out of each other's home if no one else is there.

◆ Avoid alcohol and drugs.

◆ Don't allow anyone to touch you where you do not want them to. Demand that the person stop. Sexual assault is a crime. Threaten to press charges. Demand to be taken home immediately or leave on your own and go to where there are other people. Call for help.

74
—

AIDS seems so out of control. I'm worried about becoming infected. Should I be? What does the church teach about AIDS?

The pandemic of AIDS (Acquired Immune Deficiency Syndrome) is the scourge of modern times, this era's equivalent to the plague of the Dark Ages. Its cause is HIV (the human immunodeficiency virus), which attacks certain white blood cells, termed T-cells. Eventually, this virus destroys a person's immune system, causing the individual to suffer a host of diseases a healthy immune system would normally reject.

In time, an *opportunistic infection* (for example, a rare cancer like Kaposi's sarcoma) will kill the person. To date, there is no known cure for AIDS, though certain drugs like AZT can slow its progression.

At present there are only four known ways to become infected by the AIDS virus: (1) through sexual contact (oral, anal, or vaginal sexual contact); (2) through blood transfusions contaminated with HIV; (3) through sharing dirty needles (shooting drugs, tattooing, body piercing, etc.); (4) through the birth process (there is up to a one-in-two possibility that an HIV positive mother will infect her baby).

Common to all these ways of transmission of the HIV is the sharing of body fluids, especially semen, vaginal secretions, and contaminated blood. You cannot become infected through casual contact like touching or hugging, using common bathroom facilities, or shaking someone's hand.

What is especially insidious about the HIV is that it may take years (even more than ten) before any symptoms of AIDS appear. In the meantime, an unsuspecting carrier can be spreading the virus to other people. Hence the crucial warning: *Having sex with one person is having sex with every one of that person's sexual partners.*

The church has taken some strong stands on the AIDS pandemic. First, the church advocates honest public discussion of the direct link between sexual activity and intravenous drug use and the transmission of HIV. Not to talk openly about this link is dishonest and unfair to those who are at risk of contacting the virus. As a moral teacher, the church also heartily endorses education that helps people choose right behavior and encourages them to make correct choices. Jesus taught personal responsibility, and so does the church.

Second, the church urges compassion for persons with AIDS. In a directive entitled *Called to Compassion and Responsibility: A Response to the HIV-AIDS Crisis* (1989) the American bishops write:

> Persons with AIDS are not distant, unfamiliar people. . . . We must . . . embrace them with unconditional love. The Gospel demands reverence for life in all circumstances. Compassion—love—toward persons infected with HIV is the only authentic gospel response.

In addition, in *The Many Faces of AIDS: A Gospel Response* (1987), the American bishops teach that stereotyping, prejudice, anger, recrimination, rejection, and isolation are all un-Christian responses to persons with AIDS. They also remind those who are HIV positive to live responsibly so as not to expose others to the disease.

Without condoning self-destructive behavior or denying personal responsibility, we must reject the idea that this illness is a direct punishment by God.

> ~ *Called to Compassion and Responsibility:*
> *A Response to the HIV-AIDS Crisis,*
> United States Bishops

75

Condoms are a proven and accepted tool for preventing the spread of *AIDS* and other sexually transmitted diseases. Why doesn't the church allow the use of condoms?

Actually condoms are not a proven and accepted tool for preventing the transmission of AIDS and other STDs. Although condoms do somewhat lessen the risk of being infected with HIV when a person has sex with a person who is HIV-positive, they do not eliminate the risk to an acceptable level. *The medical truth is that condoms fail more than 30 percent of the time in preventing the transmission of*

HIV. Since AIDS is *always* fatal, it is simply insane to risk a one-out-of-three chance of dying. Would you play Russian roulette with a six-chamber gun loaded with two bullets? The church is into truth-telling. It would be wrong for the church to engage in the deception of special interest groups that promote the use of condoms to the detriment of your health and the risk of your life. It would be wrong for the church to lie and tell you to use condoms contrary to church teaching in union with God's plan. It would be wrong for the church to tell teens that they cannot control their sex drive. The church has too much respect for both the truth and for you to participate in these falsehoods.

The task of the church, as Christ's presence in our midst, is to call us to be the people who God created us to be. The church's mission also reminds us that we should act in harmony with God's plan for us. This includes using our sexuality in a moral way.

Sexual intercourse is a gift which God has given to us to show love in a profound, unconditional way and to procreate new life. This full sexual sharing can take place morally only in the marriage of a man and woman who publicly pledge their undying commitment to each other.

In teaching Christ's law on human sexuality, the church calls us to live *chastely.* Chastity is the virtue that empowers us to use our sexuality in a way that is consistent with our state in life. For unmarried people, *abstaining* from sexual intercourse is the chaste, God-intended way to relate to others sexually. Abstinence is moral. And abstinence is fail-proof "safe sex."

Sex engaged in contrary to God's plan always brings hurt. Sex that results in AIDS kills. Unmarried sexual intercourse may also break hearts. It can cause self-shame and can lower self-esteem. It always carries spiritual guilt because it alienates one from God and others. It can result in feelings of being used. The list goes on and on. Abstinence, on the other hand, will *not* hurt you. In fact, it could save your life.

Why don't Catholics know more about the Bible?
Who do Protestants know it better?

Why can't women be priests?

Did the church always have priests? Do we need
priests t

Why can

Is it tru
know sor
allowed?

What is
pope can

Why is
really w
do?

I have do
ings. I a
calls sin
we all co
thing wr

How does
and who

Why do

As a little kid I used to love to hear about my
guardian angel. What's the truth about angels?
Do I really have a guardian angel?

What is purgatory?

Why doesn't the church stay out of politics?

Chapter

5

Catholic Headlines on the Front Page

Issues of Controversy, Confusion, and Concern

*Y*ou may have seen the story on one of the afternoon talk shows: *Woman claims to have been secretly married to a Catholic priest for over eighteen years.* When the man's religious order discovered the marriage, she said, they asked him to make a choice. The seventy-year-old priest gave up his marriage and returned to his religious community!

Whether true or not, church teaching and rules—in this case its requirement of celibacy for priests—have lent themselves to scrutiny and wonder by those within and outside of the church. Many of these issues have made the front page of the newspaper or the lead story on the evening news.

This chapter takes up some of the controversial topics in today's church—Catholics' knowledge of the Bible, married priests, women priests, nuns, the role of Mary, and

the belief in guardian angels. It concludes with a discussion
of "the last things": judgment, purgatory, and heaven and
hell. Subjects that should probably be on the front page
more often.

76

—

Why don't Catholics know more about the Bible? Why do Protestants know it better?

Before the invention of the Gutenberg press in the fif-
teenth century, bibles were scarce. Also, most people were
illiterate. For those reasons alone very few people were
able to read the Bible. Historically there was also a time
when church leaders did discourage ordinary Catholics
from reading the Bible. This was especially true after the
Protestant Reformation took hold in sixteenth-century
Europe.

After the Protestant Reformation, bishops and pastors
feared that uneducated lay people might misinterpret the
Bible if they read it own their own. Certainly, a misreading
and twisting of certain Bible passages contributed to the
formation of various Protestant denominations. Catholics
naturally looked to their leaders for interpretation of the
Bible.

While ordinary Catholics distrusted the Bible, terming
it that "Protestant book," many Protestants turned their
backs on Catholic tradition, teaching, and various forms of
worship, including the sacraments. For many Protestants,
reading the Bible became their major contact with God.

Mastering the Bible's content became the prime goal of Protestant religious education.

Thankfully, today's Catholics have become more aware of their duty to learn from and pray with the Word of God. And an increasingly number of Protestant churches are appreciating anew the mystery and beauty of Catholic ritual forms.

Merely occasionally sampling the Word of God will never give you a taste for it. St. Jerome, the translator of the famous Latin Vulgate version of the Bible, said, "Ignorance of the scriptures is ignorance of Christ."

Since the Second Vatican Council, the church has heartily endorsed Bible study.

This sacred Synod earnestly and specifically urges all the Christian faithful . . . to learn by frequent reading of the divine Scriptures "the excelling knowledge of Jesus Christ" *(Dogmatic Constitution on Divine Revelation,* #25).

The church cherishes the written Word of God by highlighting it in the first part of the Mass, the liturgy of the word. Over the course of the three liturgical cycles, Catholics hear and reflect on large and important parts of the Bible at Mass. And all effective Catholic religious education programs today, regardless of the age-level, include a strong scripture study component.

One final thought: We learn the Bible by reading it. One person has estimated that it takes only 18 hours and 20 minutes to read the entire New Testament. And it only takes 2 hours and 45 minutes to read Luke's gospel. If you spend only ten minutes a day, you could read all of Luke in less than seventeen days. Why not give it a try?

77

Why can't women be priests?

This has been a hotly debated issue in the church in recent times. Many other Christian denominations have women clergy. Even the Anglican church—like the Roman Catholic church in many ways—has authorized the ordination of women.

Supporters of women's ordination believe that this is a church tradition—like the celibacy rule for priests—that can change to accommodate today's women who feel called to ordination. They also hold that baptized women—like men—can signify Christ to the community. Any cultural reasons for forbidding women priests in the past are not applicable today, they maintain. Therefore, they reason, the church should allow women to serve as priests.

Despite these arguments, the church teaches that it *cannot* ordain women to the priesthood. Jesus, though he stressed the dignity of women against many repressive laws of his own day, chose only male apostles. Jesus did not even include his mother, Mary, among the apostles, the forerunners of the bishops. The apostles imitated Jesus' example when they chose only male collaborators to succeed them in their ministry (CCC, #1577).

Church teaching also stresses that sacramental signs—both persons and objects—should represent what they signify by natural resemblance. The priest is a perceptible sign, "another Christ." He represents Jesus when he presents to God the prayer of the church, especially the eucharistic sacrifice (CCC, #1552). Because Christ was a male, the priest must be a male.

Priesthood is a gift that Jesus Christ gives to his church. It is not a right which anyone deserves, but a call by God to serve the church in a particular way (*CCC*, #1578). Many other ministries are open to women and men (including teens). Through baptism, we become members of Christ's body, sharing a basic dignity as God's adopted daughters and sons. The Holy Spirit showers us with many gifts, especially the gift of love, which enables us to live and serve as Christ's brothers and sisters.

The church believes these reasons reflect Christ's intention concerning ordination. To clear up confusion, Pope John Paul II told the world's bishops in a "definitive statement" in 1994 that the church has no authority to ordain women to the priesthood.

What Do You Think?

◆ What is a church ministry you feel called to?

◆ How do you see yourself serving the church ten years from now?

78

Did the church always have priests? Do we need priests today?

In his own earthly ministry, Jesus selected twelve apostles to help him in his mission of preaching God's kingdom. After his resurrection, he commissioned his disciples to carry the gospel to the four corners of the world (Mt 8:19-20).

As the early church developed and its needs grew, a hierarchical form of leadership emerged. The tasks of bishops, priests, and deacons—as they are today—included the following:

♦ to pass on the true faith and instruct people in it,

♦ to lead people in prayer and in the celebration of the sacraments, especially the eucharist,

♦ to coordinate service efforts, especially those for the poor.

A priest is a mediator between God and people. Jesus is the one, true Priest who leads us to God and makes it possible for us to approach the all-holy One. By virtue of our baptism, every Christian shares in Christ's mission of bringing God to people and people to God. You, too, have an invaluable *priestly* ministry of being Christ for others.

The function of the *ordained* priesthood is to support each of us in our own Christian ministry of proclaiming, celebrating, and serving the gospel. Every complex organization needs officials to guarantee that essential tasks get done. Scripture and tradition show the wisdom of having ordained bishops, priests, and deacons to guide and instruct us and to serve as overseers, preachers, teachers, and leaders.

79

Why can't priests marry?

The requirement for non-married priesthood—clerical celibacy—in the Roman Catholic church is not a divine law. Nothing in Jesus' teaching reveals that he *required* priests to remain unmarried. Peter himself had a wife (see Mk 1:30). And tradition holds that all the apostles, except for John, had wives and families.

Though Jesus did not require celibacy, it can be said that he did strongly *encourage* it (Mt 19:10f, Mk 10:29, and Lk 14:26) for those who commit themselves totally to the spread of God's kingdom. Celibate priests do, in fact, follow the example of Jesus himself, who remained unmarried for the sake of God's kingdom.

St. Paul also counseled celibacy (1 Cor 7:32ff) so persons could completely devote themselves to serving God's people.

Finally, priestly celibacy is a "sign of contradiction" to the world. It reminds us that in eternity there will be no marriage. We will all be one in a loving union with God. The celibate priest is a living symbol in the present world of the future world that awaits all God's people.

What is the history of the celibacy rule for priests? The Western church (or Latin rite), from the earliest centuries, highly valued priestly celibacy. Thus in 306, the local council of Elvira in Spain issued a law requiring a celibate clergy. Gradually, other local councils enforced priestly celibacy. Finally, the Second Lateran Council in 1139 adopted a celibate priesthood for the entire Western, Latin-rite church.

The Eastern church, made up of various rites (e.g., the Byzantine rite) in communion with the pope, permits a married man to be ordained a deacon or priest. But the Eastern rites forbid a priest to marry *after* ordination. They also require that bishops remain unmarried.

You may have read that the pope has accepted some married Anglican and Episcopalian clergy as priests in the Catholic church. The pope extends this special dispensation to certain converts so they can continue serving as official ministers after becoming Catholics. Since the celibacy rule is not a divine law, the holy father can make exceptions when circumstances warrant.

With the shortage of priests, many are calling for optional celibacy for today's priesthood. There are many good arguments pro and con on this issue. Current church leadership, however, argues that celibacy is a valuable gift God has given to the church for undivided service for God's kingdom.

80

Is it true, "once a priest, always a priest"? Yet I know some men leave the priesthood. Is this allowed? Why do they leave?

Why do priests leave? It's hard to generalize but national surveys have unveiled some common reasons, including the following:

◆ *"Burnout" that leads to unmanageable stress.* This type of stress can result in the loss of idealism, the lack of energy, and the lessening of a sense of purpose. There are many demands on priests (and religious). Some leave the active ministry because of these demands, many of them unrealistic.

◆ *Problems with the promise of celibacy.* Several studies show that the celibacy rule for priests is a major reason why many young men today do not consider ordained ministry or leave after ordination.

◆ *Low morale.* This is often caused by overwork, "bad press" (for example, reports of sexual abuse cases involving priests), and a lack of support and appreciation from those they serve.

◆ *Loneliness.* This is a key factor especially for parish priests who do not live a communal life.

◆ *Problems with church authority or teaching.* This often leads to unwillingness to support church teachings or policies. For some, leaving is the more honest option.

◆ *A secular society.* Materialism, consumerism, status, and other "values" promoted and praised by today's society weaken some priest's religious commitment.

◆ *Lack of an active, vigorous prayer life.* Without a solid prayer life, faith can weaken. And with weakened faith, commitments can begin to crumble.

It is true that the sacrament of holy orders makes a man a priest forever, hence the saying, "Once a priest, always a priest." However, the church does offer a process called *laicization* that dispenses priests from their vows and allows them to leave the active ministry and return to the lay state. A laicized priest may no longer serve in any liturgical capacity or administer a Catholic school. In an emergency situation, however, a laicized priest can exercise his priestly ministry. For example, if he confronts a life-threatened accident victim on a deserted road, he may hear the person's confession.

Remember, those in full-time, active ministry need your love, understanding, and support. Take the time to thank and compliment them. Above all, pray for them. We need them to serve us and to challenge us by their own example to live the gospel. They deserve our gratitude.

81

—

What is papal infallibility? Does this mean the pope can't make any mistakes?

Author John Deedy recounts the story of Cardinal James Gibbons of Baltimore, who had just returned from Rome. A reporter asked Cardinal Gibbons if he thought the pope was infallible. Gibbons replied, "All I know is that he kept referring to me as 'Jibbons.'"[1]

The pope at the time was the Italian Leo XIII who, as Italians do, pronounced "g" as "j." The story may not be true. But it does tell us that papal infallibility does not mean the pope is perfect. He can make mistakes in his private opinions. And, as a man, he can sin.

Papal infallibility refers to the spirit of truth, a charism or gift which Jesus gave to the church. It results from Jesus' promise to Peter that he would never permit "the gates of the underworld" to overpower the church (see Mt 16:16-19). In this gift, Jesus does not allow the church, in its *official* teaching on faith and morals, to betray the vision he has entrusted to it.

The Christian community originally gave great respect to the teachings of the apostles and later to the local churches founded by the apostles. From the fourth century on special respect was given the church of Rome and its bishop, since this was the place of St. Peter's death and his community.

In 1870, the First Vatican Council declared the infallibility of the pope an official church dogma. It stated that the pope is only infallible when he invokes the highest authority of his office, that is, when he teaches *ex cathedra* (from the chair of Peter). Furthermore, the pope and bishops speak infallibly only on *traditional* teachings, doctrines that the church has always taught and believed. They cannot invent new doctrines. They can only solemnly define teachings that have been part of the church's heritage. There have only been two papal infallible statements declared since in the last 150 years: the Immaculate Conception of Mary (1854) and the Assumption of Mary into Heaven (1950).

82

Why is Mary so important to Catholics? Do we really worship her as some people say Catholics do?

Catholics, like all Christians, worship and adore God alone. To worship anyone or anything else is to commit *idolatry*, forbidden by the first commandment. But Catholics do *venerate* ("to regard with respect") Mary and the saints because of their wholehearted love and service of God and their holiness of life. We give Mary greater reverence than the other saints because she is the queen of the saints, the Mother of God. She is also our mother because Jesus gave her to the church when he told the beloved disciple John "Behold your mother" (Jn 19:27) as he hung dying on the cross.

When we admire Mary, God's great masterpiece, we are honoring the Divine Artist. Mary herself proclaimed, "The Almighty has done great things for me. Holy is his name (Lk 1:49).

When we venerate Mary and the saints, we are not praying to them. Rather, we are praying in solidarity with them. Because they are our ancestors in the faith, they pray alongside us, interceding for us before God. Mary is a powerful intercessor. The incident at Cana—where Jesus changed water into wine because Mary requested him do so—shows how valuable a loving mother's intercession can be. For centuries, Catholics have recognized the power of Mary's help whenever they recite the Hail Mary. In this prayer we petition Mary to "pray for us sinners now and at the hour of our death."

We also honor Mary and the saints when we try to imitate their holy lives, especially their virtues. Mary deserves special honor because she exemplified the Christian virtues *par excellence*. For example:

◆ *Mary brought God to humanity, the task of all Christians.* She showed the way by being a perfect example of faith. Not knowing how or even why, she said "yes" to God's invitation to be the mother of Jesus. In the Lord's Prayer we pray, "Thy will be done." Mary perfectly shows how to achieve this.

◆ *Mary remained faithful her entire life.* Her commitment to the Lord was not a flash in the pan. She stayed the course, even in the extremely difficult days of her son's passion and death. Mary embodies the meaning of discipleship.

◆ *Mary was humble.* The most blessed of all women and men, she gave God credit for what God accomplished through her. She *praised* God unceasingly. All we are and all we have are pure gifts from a loving God. Mary teaches us how to say thanks to our incredibly generous Father.

◆ *Mary lived only to know, love, and serve God.* Our faith teaches that our primary goal in life is to know, love, and serve God in this life and to join the Triune God in an eternity of perfect happiness. Mary lived her life in a sinless, exemplary way, doing what God calls us all to do. She deserves our respect, honor, veneration, and imitation.

83

—

I have doubts about several of the church's teachings. I also know people who do what the church calls sinful (for example, premarital sex). Yet we all consider ourselves Catholics. Is there anything wrong with that?

One important aspect of faith is trust. And trust involves risk. If this were not so, faith would not be faith but knowledge. At your age, believing in church teachings requires trust in the reliable testimony of prior generations of Catholics. It also means trusting that Jesus remains with the church, guiding and directing it in truth.

A certain amount of questioning, confusion, and uncertainty, and even difficulty with this or that aspect of Catholic teaching is normal, and this is certainly true for teens who are trying to make the Catholic faith their own. In fact, questioning can be a sign of maturity, a desire to understand church teaching, some of which directly oppose today's secular values and "truisms."

What should you do? First, believe that our Lord will strengthen you as you seek the truth about him and his church. Pray for his help. Be confident that he will help you preserve the gift of faith which he has given to you. Second, be humble enough to admit that you don't know everything. Consult the wisdom of teachers in the church, those trained to help you understand the truths of the faith. This would include parish priests and religious educators. Third, be patient with yourself. Try to live as a faithful disciple of Jesus. With Christian living comes Christian understanding.

Concerning the second part of your statement: don't forget that *all* Catholics are sinners. Remember, Jesus came to minister to sinners, to be the Divine Physician to those who need healing. The church is not an exclusive club for saints, but a hospital for sinners.

A further question remains: Are the people you spoke of willing to seek repentance if they come to understand that their behavior is sinful? People who persist in a life of sin, without being sorry and making a firm purpose to amend their lives with God's help, are insincere. Jesus himself said,

> *I*t is not anyone who says to me, "Lord, Lord,"
> who will enter the kingdom of heaven, but the
> person who does the will of my Father in heaven
> (Mt 7:21).

The issue you raise is actually more serious for adult Catholics who for whatever reason have labeled themselves "cafeteria Catholics." They choose only those teachings of Christ and his church they wish to believe and follow. Jesus did not found a smorgasbord or cafeteria church where a person can pick and choose what to believe and what not to believe. Dining at his table means digesting all his church's teachings. It means making an honest, even heroic, effort at putting them into practice.

And, if we fall short, it means asking for the Lord's forgiveness and striving, with his help, to be faithful to him in the future.

---

*T*en thousand difficulties do not make one doubt.
~Cardinal John Henry Newman

What Do You Say?

Agree or disagree. People don't leave the church because they have an intellectual difficulty with a particular church teaching. They often leave because they are behaving immorally and don't want to hear the truth about their sinful lives.

84

—

How does the church decide who becomes a saint and who doesn't?

The church sets aside All Saints' Day, November 1, to honor the countless anonymous saints who are with the Lord in heaven. These are the "uncanonized" saints. Undoubtedly, among these millions of saints are many of your own relatives from past generations. If their faith and love were heroic while here on earth, you can be sure they are in heaven. This is the day of the liturgical year when the church remembers their lives.

Canonization is the official process the church uses to declare a person is in heaven and may be honored as a saint. Today, this process is long, involved, and costly. In brief, it involves three steps:

1. Supporters in a local diocese nominate a candidate's name after his or her death by petitioning the bishop to investigate the person's qualifications for sainthood. If the bishop, and later the Sacred Congregation for the Causes of Saints, conclude that the person had heroic virtues, then the church declares the person "Venerable."

2. Stage two carefully examines the person's life and writings to make sure they conform to Catholic teaching. This step involves interviewing known living acquaintances of the saint. For the process to proceed, it must show that praying to the candidate resulted in one miracle because of his or her intercession. If the candidate passes this stage, the church declares the person "Blessed." This means Catholics can venerate this person within a certain geographical area or in the religious community to which he or she belonged.

3. Step three involves an exhaustive examination of the candidate's life by the Congregation for the Causes of the Saints. If the candidate passes this test, a commission of bishops and cardinals may present the cause to the pope. If the pope approves, he will issue a Bull of Canonization which proclaims the person a saint of the Catholic church. At this stage Catholics may honor this saint publicly throughout the world. Bishops can name churches after the saint. And the church may assign a liturgical feast day to the newly canonized saint.

As you can see, the process of canonization is complex. You may have noticed that many canonized saints belong to religious orders. Does this mean that lay people, like married couples, are not worthy of sainthood? No! The practical reason is that religious orders have the financial means and "staying power" to promote the cause of a particular candidate over a long time period.

Most saints are, in fact, anonymous. It is the hope of the church that one day Christians will also pray to and honor you. Christ calls each person to be a saint. He wants us to live our ordinary lives in an extraordinary way by loving and serving him through others. As the song goes, may you be "in their number when the saints go marching in."

85

Why do we pray to the saints?

Think of all Christians as members of one big family. This family—called the communion of saints—includes those of us still alive on earth, as well as those in heaven or in purgatory. Death does not destroy our spiritual relationship with each other. In fact, it can intensify the relationship because our friends and relatives in heaven care for us very much and can intercede for us before God.

When we pray "to" the saints we are really asking them to pray *with* us and *for* us to our Lord Jesus, our unique mediator and savior. All graces and salvation come through him alone.

The saints led heroic lives of holiness on earth. They gave God great honor when they lived among us. They continue to inspire us to imitate their example. When we pray to them for intercession, we are rejoicing with them. We unite our own prayers with theirs, praying to Jesus, who takes all of our petitions to God the Father.

Jesus told of the special power of joining our prayer to that of others (Mt 18:19-20). The New Testament frequently instructs us to pray for each other (e.g., Jas 5:16). Undoubtedly, you have often asked others to pray for you because you recognize the spiritual power of several voices joined in prayer. When you pray with the saints you show that you firmly believe that our union with the members of Christ's family goes beyond death.

86

As a little kid I used to love to hear about my guardian angel. What's the truth about angels? Do I really have a guardian angel?

The church does indeed teach as a truth of faith the existence of spiritual, non-bodily beings called angels. With a nature superior to that of humans, angels have two key roles: to serve God and to be God's messengers. The word *angel* means "messenger."

As beings of pure spirit, angels have free will and intelligence. They are personal and immortal creatures of God, far surpassing in splendor any of God's visible creatures (*CCC*, #330).

The Bible mentions angels more than three hundred times. Judaism, Christianity, and Islam all believe in angels and even agree on the names of three of them: Michael, Gabriel, and Raphael.

Church tradition, drawing on scriptural revelation (1 Col 1:16 and Rm 8:38), lists nine "choirs" or classes of angels. In ascending order they are: angels, archangels, principalities, powers, virtues, dominations, thrones, cherubim, and seraphim.

Today there is great interest in angels, with many popular books and TV specials devoted to them. This reflects, undoubtedly, a contemporary society searching for spiritual values. But Catholics have always held devotion to angels in high regard. As a matter of course, your grandparents, and perhaps even your parents, learned to pray with their guardian angels.

Yes, the church holds that each person has a guardian angel. It bases that teaching on Old Testament references such as the angel Raphael protecting Tobias in the Book of Tobit. And Jesus himself speaks of guardian angels when he warned people not to give scandal to children (Mt 18:10). The job of guardian angels is to guard and protect us. Some saints, for example, St. Frances of Rome, claim to have seen and conversed daily with their guardian angels.

When tempted, invoke your angel. He is more eager to help you than you are to be helped! Ignore the devil and do not be afraid of him: he trembles and flees at your guardian angel's sight.

~St. John Bosco[2]

87

What is purgatory?

Purgatory is the spiritual state of purification of those souls who die in God's grace and friendship, yet are not free from all the imperfection of sin (CCC, 1030-1032). In the state of purgatory, these souls endure punishment for unforgiven venial sins and already forgiven mortal sins. Since nothing that is imperfect can go before God (see, for example, Wis 7:35 and Hb 1:13), this purification prepares souls to meet the all-holy Lord face-to-face in heaven.

The church has wisely not defined the time, intensity, or quality of the punishments which the souls in purgatory experience. Once we die, we enter eternity—God's time. Thus, to talk about purgatory in human terms like time is not very helpful. All we know is that through this process a person becomes perfectly unselfish and capable of loving God fully. Thus, a transformed friend of the Lord can meet God with a pure heart. Any pain associated with this process is the pain of wanting to become worthy of union with a perfect, all-loving God.

Scripture teaches that prayers for the dead can help deliver them from the remnants of their sins (2 Mc 12:38-46). This underscores the doctrine of the communion of saints, the bond of unity that exists between God's people on earth and those who have died.

The church has always offered prayers for the dead, especially at the eucharist. Almsgiving, works of penance, and indulgences are other practices that the church has supported as valuable helps to our departed ancestors in purgatory.

88

—

Why doesn't the church stay out of politics?

Because the church lacks political power, it cannot force people or governments to act one way rather than another.

But the church does have the duty to teach in Christ's name. It can persuade Catholics and other open-minded people to consider seriously the requirements of the gospel.

Note some of the problems facing us today: equal rights for women, fairness for workers, prejudice against persons of color, abortion, assisted suicide, euthanasia, poverty, environmental pollution, wars in various places around the world. These and many other local, state, national, and international issues beg for an intelligent and Christian response.

The church is the body of Christ, his presence in the world. As the Lord taught his followers to love and care for the "least of these" in their midst, so must the church today follow his example.

Jesus revealed that all people have tremendous worth and dignity as children of God. Thus, the church must continually call people to respect everyone's basic dignity. It *must* judge social, economic, and political matters, especially when persons' rights and their salvation require it.

Church social justice teaching of the past one hundred years proceeds from the principle that basic economic and political rights flow from our dignity as persons. This teaching includes certain principles of reflection, criteria for judging, and guidelines for action. For example, church social teaching condemns any theory that makes the disordered desire for money the basis of an economy. It also condemns any system that would reduce a human being to a mere means of profit. The first evil leads to materialism and consumerism. The second evil destroys the individual dignity of persons.

Issues of the economy and politics entwine. They result from real people making real decisions. Hence, the church asks people to reflect on basic questions. For example, in the area of economics, we should ask: What does the economy do *for* people? What does it do *to* people? And how do people *participate*? By asking these questions, the church challenges people to act responsibly in the social order to make laws and set up policies that protect human rights.

As Christ's representative, the church must especially speak out for the poor, the powerless, and the defenseless. This includes watching out for the rights of the unborn and needy people at home and abroad. It also means speaking out for minorities who are receiving unjust treatment in a political or economic system controlled by the wealthy.

Though it would not be advisable for the church to form political parties, the church must teach in Christ's name. It must promote justice, the virtue of fairness that gives persons their due as children of a loving God. Like a good mother looking out for her children, the church also encourages her sons and daughters to participate actively in the political and economic arenas. Lay people especially have a key role to play in promoting justice in the political system.

What Do You Say?

- Is it moral for us to keep for our own exclusive use what we don't need when others lack the basic requirements for a decent life? Explain.

- Is it moral to work to abolish welfare programs for the poor? Explain.

How should I pray?

Do my prayers affect God? For example, can they get God to change his mind?

God never answers my prayers, so why should I bother praying?

What are Jesus' most important teachings? How should I respond to them?

How

Whe

Wha

How

Can

I wa
really

I don
Wha

How can I decide the best course for my life? Right now, I have no idea.

How do I know if I have a religious vocation?

What can I do to keep in touch with my Catholic faith when I go to college?

In the last analysis, how will God decide whether or not I get into heaven?

Chapter

6

Doing the Right Thing

God's Plan for My Life

What does God have in mind for you? Certainly at this stage of your life your future is filled with many dreams and possibilities. But have you involved God in seeking to determine the directions for your life? How do you see your Christian discipleship interwoven into your chosen path? Consider these challenging words from St. Teresa of Avila as an integral part of any option:

> *Christ has no body now but yours,*
> *No hands, no feet on earth but yours.*
> *Yours are the eyes through*
> *which he looks,*
> *compassion on this world.*
> *Yours are the feet with which he walks to*
> *do good.*

189

Yours are the hands with which
he blesses all the world.

Yours are the hands.
Yours are the feet.
Yours are the eyes.
You are his body.

This concluding chapter takes up many questions about how to grow in the Christian life—questions about Jesus' teaching, prayer, vocation, decision-making, and college. As you read them, consider other questions you may have about your faith. Be sure to seek out answers from other Catholic Christians whom you respect and trust.

89

How should I pray?

Your question shows that you consider prayer to be very important. And it is. It is to the spiritual life and friendship with God what water and food are to physical life. The sign outside the church has it just about right: "Seven days without prayer makes one weak." Or, as one perceptive person remarked, "Prayer is a way of life, not just a case of emergency."

The first step in prayer is to find a regular time for it. (You always make time for what is important, and prayer is important.) Next, find a special place for prayer. Distractions are the plague of regular pray-ers. Finding a good place to pray—your bedroom, a chapel or church, a

scenic place outside—can help cut down (but never eliminate) distractions that will inevitably come along.

The next step is to calm yourself down for the purpose
of focusing on your prayer. Let the cares of the day drain
away. You may wish to relax by doing deep breathing exer-
cises. An agitated body leads to an agitated spirit at prayer.

When you are ready to begin your prayer time, try the
following:

◆ Become aware of God's presence all around you.
  God holds you in the palm of his hand. You are
  always in God's mind. You are like a fish swim-
  ming in an ocean of God's love.

◆ Approach God as you would a friend. God *is*
  your friend, and prayer is essentially a conversation with the greatest friend you'll ever have. It
  involves talking and listening.

◆ In the *talking* part of your prayer, praise and thank
  God for all the gifts you've been given: life,
  friends, health, talents. Also express to God your
  sorrow for your sins, your mistakes, your lack of
  attention to other people and God. Believe that
  God, like any good friend, forgives and accepts
  you. God won't dwell on your past failings, and
  neither should you. Just ask the Lord for the
  strength to continue to be and do better.

◆ Now you are ready to take your concerns to the
  Lord. Jesus told us to petition God often and to be
  persistent in doing so. Speak to God simply as a
  child would to a loving parent. Ask the Lord for
  "daily bread"—what you need physically, psychologically, and spiritually. Remember to pray for
  your family, your friends and relatives, the poor
  and the needy, as well as for your enemies.

◆ Prayer also involves *listening* to God. Ask the
  Lord to speak to you. Look over your past day—

the people, the events, the successes and the failures, the joys and the sadness. Ask God to reveal
to you more of their meaning in the overall context of your life. Stop and listen to your life. Is
God telling you to slow down, to stop worrying,
to be more generous? Some people find it helpful
to read from one of the gospels or epistles, stop-
ping periodically to let God's word speak to
their hearts. You might also want to try reading
from other scriptures or some other spiritual
book during this listening part of your prayer.

◆ Enjoy God's presence around you—"basking in
the sunshine of God's love"—without thinking
in words at all. St. Jean Vianney tells of a saintly
old peasant who reported on his prayer life: "I
don't say anything to God. I just sit and look at
him and let him look at me."

You might conclude your prayer with a promise or
pledge to God. For example, you might tell God you are
going to enjoy the beautiful world around you by taking a
walk and noticing all the bright colors. Or you might make
a point to be more considerate of those you meet during the
day. You might also promise to say quiet prayers of love to
the Lord at different times during the day, for example as
you begin each class at school.

90

---

*Do my prayers affect God? For example,
can they get God to change his mind?*

Prayer brings together two great mysteries. The first is of an eternally loving God who knows all that was, all that is, and all that ever will be. The second involves the mystery of our own free will, which enables us to accept or reject God's invitation to love.

When we pray, we are praying to a loving God who has known our prayers from all eternity. Thus, when we pray we are not telling God anything "new." Nor do we exercise any power over God, for example, the power to persuade God to change his mind about something. In fact, it is the Holy Spirit who first inspired us to pray. As a result of knowing and inspiring our prayers from all eternity, God has included them in the plan for the world. Furthermore, the very prayers God knew we would ask have been answered!

Therefore, prayer does not change God. Prayer changes us. Prayer is essential for the Christian life because it makes us reflect on our needs and turn to the One who can fulfill those needs. It helps us understand God's great love for us. It helps us become more grateful. It helps us realize that we must accept God's will. And prayer strengthens us to do God's will. In short, when we pray, we allow the mystery of a loving God to touch and change us.

Jesus knew the power that prayer has of conforming us to God. This is why he himself prayed often throughout his life, showing both how and why to pray. Jesus revealed that some of God's activity in the world relies on our free and open response to it. For example, God's love is not forced on you. God offers it to you as a wonderful gift which you can accept or reject. Prayer helps you recognize the invitation. It opens you up to God's activity. It heightens your awareness of God's hidden but powerful presence in everything around you. It helps you see that God will give you many gifts if you pray. As Jesus said, if you don't ask, you won't get.

We learn how to pray from Jesus, the teacher of prayer *par excellence*. He told us to pray often, both alone and with others. He instructed us to be open to God and to pray with childlike faith. He taught us to trust that our God—like a loving parent—will give us what is good for us.

Jesus also encouraged us to be persistent in our prayers and to pray with forgiveness in our hearts. If we harbor grudges, our hearts will be hard and the warmth of God's love will not touch us. If we follow Jesus' example and his advice on how to pray, God will indeed change us and answer our prayers.

Read and Reflect

Read Luke 11:1-13. *Reflect* on what this passage tells you about prayer.

91

God never answers my prayers, so why should I bother praying?

Jesus told the parable of the Persistent Widow (Lk 18:1-8) to remind us of the importance of the virtue of patience in praying. We can't be like the person who said, "Dear Lord, help me be patient—*right now!*" God answers our prayers, but in God's time, not ours.

Sometimes we don't receive the desired answer. Often it has to with a lack of faith. St. James writes:

*P*rayer must be made with faith, and no trace of doubt, because a person who has doubts is like the waves thrown up in the sea by the buffeting of the wind. That sort of person, in two minds, inconsistent in every activity, must not expect to receive anything from the Lord (Jas 1:6-8).

The antidote to doubtful prayer is the example of the father who begged Jesus to cure his child: "I have faith. Help my lack of faith!" (Mk 9:24).

At other times, we think God doesn't even hear our prayers. Yet we really fail to understand God's plans for us. God does answer our prayers, but we don't always recognize God's answer. An anonymous author put it well:

I asked for strength that I might achieve;
   He made me weak that I might obey.
I asked for health that I might do great things;
   He gave me grace that I might do better things.
I asked for riches that I might be happy;
   He gave me poverty that I might be wise.
I asked for power that I might have the praise of men;
   He gave me weakness that I might feel a need of God.
I asked for all things that I might enjoy life;
   He gave me life that I might enjoy all things.
I received nothing I had asked for;
   He gave me all I had hoped for.

Remember that God always answers *sincere* prayer. But again, God's answer might be something we don't expect. Sometimes God answers "no" to our desires because they would harm us. At other times, God helps us see that what we are praying for is something that we can accomplish on our own with gifts he has already given us. Consider, for example, the student who begs God for an "A" on a test. But the student fails to study. In this case, it's unlikely that the student will achieve the desired grade. Remember the adage, "God helps those who help themselves."

But God will always provide the superabundant gift of love to those who pray. Recall Jesus' own promise:

> *W*hat father among you, if his son asked for a fish, would hand him a snake? Or if he asked for an egg, hand him a scorpion? If you then, evil as you are, know how to give your children what is good, how much more will the heavenly Father give the Holy Spirit to those who ask him! (Lk 11:11-13).

In conclusion, please note the wise observation of Trappist Basil Pennington on prayer:

> *G*od will give us whatever we want, asking in prayer—what we truly want, not what we say we want or even think we want. God listens to the heart, not to the lips. He knows, too, how limited our understanding and knowledge are. He sees our truest desires and knows how they can best be fulfilled. And this is what he grants. We may not see it at the moment, but we will in time. . . . If God seems to be saying "No" to some prayers, it is because he is saying "Yes" to the deepest prayer of our hearts.[1]

There are three answers to prayer: Yes, No, and Wait Awhile.

Modern Parable on Prayer

A man left his Rolex in a hotel in another town. When he got home, he called the hotel. He told the manager his problem and the manager went to look for the watch. He found it, placed it in the hotel safe, and returned to the phone to tell the absent-minded caller the good news. But the caller had hung up without leaving his name.

92

What are Jesus' most important teachings? How should I respond to them?

Jesus never wrote a book, yet the libraries of the world contain more works about him and his teaching than any other historical figure. Jesus never founded a college, yet countless millions have joyfully studied and discovered life in his lessons. Jesus was a brilliant teacher. Even his contemporaries recognized as much. The telling of parables was a favorite method he used to convey his unique, memorable, and life-changing teachings. His remarkable message centered on his Father's kingdom, God's reign. Jesus taught the following lessons, each with a built-in call for a personal response:

1. *God's kingdom is here right now.* The "kingdom" or "reign" of God refers to God's liberating activity in human history. Jesus preached that God is reconciling and renewing all things through the Son. Right now! God's reign is taking place on earth as it is in heaven. Although this process of renewal appears small, like a mustard seed, God guarantees its inevitable growth. On the one hand, salvation is taking place through Jesus. On the other hand, the kingdom will reap a bounteous harvest at the end of time when the process begun in Jesus will reach its completion. We should

live our lives in the realization that we are in the presence of God and God's reign.

2. *God's kingdom is a gift, open to everyone.* God loves everyone, and reaches out especially to sinners and outcasts. Like a good shepherd, God searches for the lost sheep. Like the merciful father of the prodigal son, God joyfully and unconditionally welcomes back wayward children. God only requires that we accept his freely given love and forgive others as God has forgiven us.

3. *The gospel requires a wholehearted response.* Always prepared for Jesus' return, we should be like the person who sold every possession to buy the treasure that was hidden in a field. In short, we must be willing to sacrifice everything for God's reign.

4. *Because a new age has dawned, change your ways!* Reality is different now than it was before. Thus, we should uproot sin in our lives and ask for God's gift of forgiveness. We should develop an intimate relationship with God in prayer. We should always be confident that the Lord will answer our prayers. And we must be like God, sharing our gifts with the poor and not hoarding the many good things God has given us.

5. *Love everyone.* Jesus taught us to love everyone, even our enemies. "Love God above everything and our neighbors as ourselves," Jesus tells us. Love is not empty words but concrete acts: feeding the hungry, giving drink to the thirsty, welcoming the stranger, clothing the naked, visiting the sick and the imprisoned.

6. *Accept the challenge of the kingdom.* To follow Jesus' teaching requires sacrifice. We must pick up a cross in imitation of him. We do this when we accept the pain and suffering that comes our way. In doing so, we, like Jesus, are promised fulfillment in this life and incredible happiness in the next.

93

How should I read and interpret the Bible?

Much of the Bible deals with a time, people, and culture that are foreign to us. Therefore, it takes effort to profitably read the Bible. Thanks to the efforts of countless scholars, the scriptures have been opened so that all can *interpret* the Bible correctly.

The basic aim of *biblical interpretation* is to bring together the world of the reader and the world of the biblical text so the meaning of the text makes sense to the reader. Biblical interpretation has two essential tasks: (1) **Gathering information** about the text, and (2) **explaining** the meaning of the text.

One approach to avoid in interpreting the Bible is *biblical fundamentalism*, which interprets scripture in an absolutely *literal* way. A fundamentalist takes each text from the Bible and treats it as though its meaning is obvious and clear. This overly literal approach fails to account for changes in language over the centuries. It also overlooks the cultural differences between our age and that of biblical times and ignores the obvious inconsistencies that sometimes appear in the biblical accounts. For example, a fundamentalist has a difficult time explaining that the first chapter of Genesis says humans were the first creatures God made, while the second chapter states humans were the last beings created.

Catholics do not approach the Bible from a fundamentalist perspective. Rather, Catholics endorse the *historical-critical* method of biblical interpretation. This method tries to understand biblical texts in their original setting, discovering the intentions of the original authors. For example, the historical-critical method tries to identify what the story of the snake talking to Adam and Eve meant to the original audience. It attempts to figure out if the teller of the story meant us to take it literally. In addition, it studies similar stories from other cultures in the ancient world in an effort to try to identify their literary form.

This method of reading the Bible relies on many important historical and literary methods like textual, literary, form, and redaction criticism; transmission history; archaeology; and sociology.

Biblical scholarship is beyond the present learning of most of us. We need the help of the experts to discover the text's original meaning. But personal Bible reading can help us discover what the scriptures mean for our own lives. You can use the following five-step "Bible-reading" plan to help you apply the Bible to your own life:

> **Step 1:** Choose a readable "study Bible." It is readable if you can write, mark, underline, and high light it. It is a study Bible if it contains an introduction to each book of the Bible and has good explanatory notes in the margins or at the bottom of the page.

> **Step 2:** First Reading. Read the text. Try to get the overall picture without getting bogged down. What is taking place? What strikes you? What confuses you? What new ideas did you get?

> **Step 3:** Study the text. Go back and reread the text slowly. Be a detective. Identify the following:

◆ *Who* is speaking? Who are the other people in the story?

◆ *What* is happening? *Why?*

◆ *Where* and *when* are the action, speech, and event taking place?

Fit the passage into the larger context. For example, what happened before?

Note any questions you might have. For example, pick out words you don't understand.

Step 4: Rely on helps. There are many ways to deepen your knowledge:

◆ Look at the introductions to the particular biblical book you are reading. Fix the passage in its historical context.

◆ Check the explanatory notes given in your Bible for the meanings of specific words and confusing passages.

◆ Look for cross-references. Reading other related scripture passages will sometimes clarify the text.

◆ Consult a Bible atlas, dictionary, or commentary for more in-depth information.

Step 5: Put it all together. Ask yourself these questions:

◆ What did this passage mean to its original audience?

◆ What does this passage mean to me? For example, what does it tell me about God, myself, other people, or life in general?

94

Where is Jesus today? How can I meet him?

If you want one way to meet Jesus today, look in the mirror! Then, turn to your neighbors and see Jesus in them also. With the eyes of faith, the Holy Spirit enables us to see that we are God's adopted children. Through our baptisms, we are brothers and sisters of Jesus and, in him, brothers and sisters of one another. Here are some more clues and information about where you can meet Jesus today:

Find Jesus in yourself. Jesus lives in you! This earth-shaking truth sums up a key aspect of the gospel. The Risen Jesus has chosen to be present in the world through his disciples. Jesus says,

> *I* am the true vine,
> and my Father is the vine dresser. . . .
> I am the vine,
> you are the branches (*Jn 15:1, 5*).

Find Jesus in the church. Whenever two or three gather in his name, Jesus is present (Mt 18:20). The church is the body of Christ. Jesus is the head, you are one of the members. Baptism incorporates you into the body. You must use your individual talents to build up the body and continue Jesus' work of salvation and sanctification in the world.

Find Jesus in the sacraments. Jesus is present to through the sacred signs called the sacraments. They are concrete symbols of love.

Jesus instituted the sacraments so he can remain close to his church. The sacraments use material symbols like words, actions, and concrete signs to express the love, concern, forgiveness, and real presence of the Lord.

The eucharist is the central sacrament. It celebrates and creates Christian community. It reenacts the Paschal Mystery of God's unlimited love for you in Jesus. It challenges you to be Christ for others, to be "bread for the world."

Catholics believe that Jesus is truly present, body and blood, in the bread and wine consecrated in the eucharistic liturgy. Jesus is also present in the priest who leads the worship. He is present in the community which comes to celebrate Jesus' loving actions. Furthermore, he is present in the scripture readings proclaimed at Mass. You are called to go forth from the eucharist and share this presence of Christ with others.

Find Jesus in the Bible. Think of the Bible as the "words of the Word." The gospels, for example, contain the teachings of Jesus. God's word is a powerful sign of his presence and love. Reading the Bible often will help you meet the living Lord.

Find Jesus in prayer. To experience Jesus as a living, concerned friend means spending time communicating with him. Prayer is simply conversation with the Lord. It helps you notice his presence and allows him to influence your mind, will, imagination, feelings, and memory. Conversing with the Lord as your closest, most understanding friend reassures you of his abiding love.

Find Jesus in the weak and humble. Jesus especially identified himself with people society considered to be lowly and outcast. You can meet Jesus whenever you welcome the stranger, feed the hungry, give drink to the thirsty, or visit the sick and the imprisoned. You will *not* find Jesus if you ignore those who are lonely, the poor, the physically and mentally challenged, or old people who need your care. As Jesus says,

*I*n truth I tell you, in so far as you neglected to
do this to one of the least of these, you neglected
to do it to me (Mt 25:45).

Find Jesus in love. Scripture tells us that God is love.
When we love, we will find Christ Jesus, God's great gift of
love to us all:

*M*y dear friends, let us love each other, since
love is from God . . . . God is love (1 Jn 4:7-8,
NAB).

95

Can rich people be saved?

Jesus came to save everyone—the rich, the poor, and
those in between. In a special way, however, Jesus identified himself with the needy by becoming a marginal person
himself and by ministering to the destitute and the powerless. Furthermore, he commanded his followers to reach
out to the poor, for example, by feeding the hungry, clothing the naked, and the like (Mt 25:31ff).

Yet, Jesus did not condemn wealth as such. He had several known wealthy followers (for example, Zacchaeus,
Lazarus, and Joseph of Arimathea). But he did warn about
riches. He said: "You cannot be the slave both of God and
money" (Mt 6:24). In short, material riches can control a
person. As Jesus pointed out: "For wherever your treasure
is, there your heart will be too" (Mt 6:21).

Jesus called for all people to be "poor in spirit" (Mt 5:3). This first beatitude is meant to counteract greed. Poverty of spirit fights the natural tendency of rich people to think they are in control, that they "deserve" what they have, that they can "buy" their way into heaven. These non-gospel attitudes can make wealthy people proud and arrogant, acting as if they don't need God.

Jesus did indeed say that it is very difficult for the rich to enter the kingdom of heaven. He said it was like a camel passing through the eye of a needle (Mt 19:23-24). Thus, it is impossible for human power and treasure to get a person into heaven. But Jesus does assure us that what is impossible for humans is possible for God. Only God saves—both those who are poor *and* those who are rich. Only God can warm the hearts of the wealthy and move them to use their wealth to help others. The wealthy should have a light grasp on worldly possessions and share them responsibly with others, especially the needy. Our heavenly reward will be in proportion to what we give away on earth.

What Would You Do?

What would you do if you won $20 million in the lottery?

96

I want to "do the right thing." What does that really mean for a Christian?

What you are speaking of is *justice*. St. Thomas Aquinas described justice as the virtue where we consistently give to each person what is his or her due by right. In other words, all people have certain inalienable rights because they are created in the divine image. Justice involves respecting the rights of others in the religious, social, political, and economic areas of life.

Here are twenty ways you can "do the right thing":

1. Develop your God-given talents and then use them for the good of others.

2. Always be honest.

3. Always tell the truth.

4. Obey all just laws, including legislation on alcohol consumption and speed limits.

5. Treat with respect your classmates, coworkers, and those in authority.

6. Don't participate in gossip, especially about another's reputation.

7. Respect the property of others.

8. Give an honest day's work for an honest day's pay.

9. Be a peacemaker.

10. Identify and then try to overcome any prejudices you might have toward members of any racial or cultural group.

11. Show concern for the poor by limiting your spending habits and sharing some of your good fortune with the needy.

12. Don't waste food.

13. Participate in food drives conducted at school or in your parish.

14. Fast on occasion to identify with the hungry.

15. Volunteer at a food bank.

16. Volunteer at senior citizens' home.

17. Dispose of waste materials responsibly. For example, don't litter. Recycle when possible.

18. Pray for peace.

19. Research possible careers that directly deal with social justice (for example, local politics, social work, inner-city teaching). This may involve reading about people who worked for social justice (for example, Dorothy Day, St. Vincent de Paul).

20. Stay informed about one of the great social issues of our day. Examples abound—war, abortion, hunger, environmental issues, racism, sexism. Write letters to newspapers and politicians expressing your views on the topic.

An old Arab proverb says, "One hour of justice is worth a hundred of prayer." Philosophers have defined justice as "truth in action." A just person is one who is living honestly and correctly, doing the right thing!

What Would You Do?

Develop a plan for justice that you can enact in the next week. Develop another long-term plan you can enact in the next six months.

97

I don't particularly like people of other races. What's so wrong about that?

You've probably heard the adage, "I don't have to like you, but I do have to love you." Christians have no option in loving. We must love everyone, including those who are different, even our enemies.

"Liking" has to do with preferences, our attraction to one thing, activity, or person, rather than another. Liking the familiar is normal and natural. However, when it comes to *not liking* people, be careful.

An African-American minister once remarked, "If you don't like me because of my ignorance, that's fine. I can go to school. If you don't like me because I'm dirty, I guess that's OK. I can wash and get clean. But if you don't like me because of my skin color, then you have a problem. Your problem is with God who made me this way."

You need to ask yourself: "Why is it that I dislike people who are different? Is it because I suffer from prejudice? Am I racist?"

Racism is the erroneous belief that some humans are inherently superior and others are innately inferior simply because of race. It is a form of prejudice (a prejudgment made without enough evidence) that can result in negative and harmful practices like speaking and listening to slurs against members of another race (for example, crude jokes and characterizations), avoiding members of different racial groups, or being involved in violence toward a group. *Discrimination*—denying people their due rights on the basis or race—is another terrible effect of racism. *Genocide*—the killing of a particular race—is the worst form of racism. This crime has reared its ugly head several times in the twentieth century.

Racism is a serious sin. It is both unloving and unjust. The church has vigorously condemned all forms of discrimination against people "on the basis of their race, color, condition of life, or religion" *(Declaration on the Relationship of the Church to Non-Christian Religions, #5).*

Ambrose Bierce, the American short-story writer, defined prejudice as "a vagrant opinion without visible means of support." Examine why you don't like certain people. If it is a matter of being close-minded, you can change. Make a serious effort to get to know and even befriend a classmate or co-worker who is of a different race. Always remember there's only one race—the human race.

98

How can I decide the best course for my life? Right now, I have no idea.

I had a student who was out drinking. Inebriated, he drove his car across some railroad tracks thinking he could beat an oncoming train. He didn't. But miraculously, this boy escaped serious injury. When I talked to him about this incident, he told me his life was spared because God had a plan for his life. I agreed with him. God does have a plan for each of us. A mature Christian will try to discover it, just as you are doing.

God's will for all of us is that we should be happy. And God has revealed the secret to happiness. The starting point is to ask yourself honestly, "Do I want to be a good person? Do I want to be a person who loves?" Answer these questions with an enthusiastic "yes" and you will on your way to discerning God's specific will for you.

Jesus said, "Seek and you will find" (Mt 7:7-8). You *can't* go wrong trying to find out God's will. However, two pre-liminaries are necessary for your search. First, *make God a part of your life.* You can do this by following the commands of Christ and the church. Thus, you will be in a better position to recognize God's activity in your life. Second, *learn from Jesus.* Frequently read and reflect on the gospels. Pray

to Jesus as your best friend and as one who perfectly discovered his Father's will. He will guide you on your quest.

To these two general practices, cultivate a spirit of
prayerful reflection. Also, you may wish to follow these
suggestions:

1. *Get to know yourself.* What are your deepest inclinations and attractions? What brings you a feeling of
   peace and harmony? What jobs and careers appeal to
   you?

   Frequently ask yourself the question that St. Ignatius
   Loyola put to himself: "Where am I going and what
   for?" Are you on the right track to heaven, or are you
   going down the wrong road? If you keep your end
   goal in sight, the Lord will show you the means to get
   there.

2. *Ask for help.* Seek a wise counselor, an adult who
   knows you well. Openly discuss your dreams with
   this trusted friend. Also take to heart the advice that
   St. Paul gave his recent converts: "Test everything and
   hold on to what is good and shun every form of evil"
   (1 Thess 5:19).

3. *Be patient with yourself.* Thank God often for your
   many gifts. Ask for forgiveness when you sin. Relax.
   Reflect on these words of Blessed Francis Libermann:

   *I*n order to go to God with your heart, your
   mind must be undisturbed, indifferent. Keep it
   quiet. Do things simply, without too much analysis. If you really want to please God and intend to
   be in full agreement with His Will, you can't go
   wrong.[2]

99

How do I know if I have a religious vocation?

Every Christian has a *vocation*, that is, a "calling" to serve Christ and other people in his name. This general Christian vocation is lived out in one of four specific ways: as a single person; as a married person; as a religious who professes the vows such as chastity, obedience, and poverty; or as an ordained priest. A priest may also be a member of a religious community.

Perhaps God is calling you to be a priest, sister, or brother. This call may be subtle but also persistent. It often begins with a yearning or desire to be as close as possible with God. Your interest may also be piqued by friendship with a priest, brother, or sister who is happy and fulfilled in his or her life. Don't stifle this attraction because of what you think others might say or because you find it a bit scary.

Here are several things to do to help determine if the priesthood and/or professed religious life is for you:

◆ First, look at the type of person you are. Do you have the qualities needed to serve God as a priest or vowed religious? For example, are you basically a kind, genuine, moral person concerned about the welfare of others? Do you have a strong desire to serve Christ and his gospel? Are you unselfish, able to take direction, flexible, cooperative, loving? Are you emotionally well-balanced, of good intelligence, and physically healthy?

These are the basic qualities that the church is looking for in candidates for the priesthood or religious life. The people who interview candidates are also looking to see if they can live the vow of celibacy. At this stage, though, don't be too worried about celibacy. There will be plenty of opportunity for you to discern this vow.

Church or community officials also want to discover a person's *motives* for wanting to be a priest, sister, or brother. Service is an excellent motive. Seeking security or prestige, or escaping from loneliness or failed relationships are not good motives.

◆ Second, pray! Prayer is essential to any vocation. Discuss your heart's longings with Jesus. Ask him for insight and courage about a possible vocation.

◆ Third, if after some time your desire and yearning continue to persist, speak about your feelings with someone you admire who is already living out a similar calling. Once, this person had the same feelings as you do now. Without exerting pressure, he or she can gently direct you to which step to take next.

100

What can I do to keep in touch with my Catholic faith when I go to college?

Going away to college is all at once an exciting and frightening prospect. It is exciting because of the new-found freedom and the many choices it involves: a new roommate, deciding on an academic major, choosing class schedules, handling a budget, and the like. Furthermore, Mom and Dad are not on your back, telling you what to do and when to do it. But this new experience can also be a little scary; you may get homesick. And you may not be sure just yet that you can handle all the freedom. You might know someone who got into the party-scene at college and lasted only a semester. You wonder, "Can this happen to me?"

More than 95 percent of the nearly eight thousand students I have taught in my twenty-eight years of teaching went on to college, survived, and are now pursuing careers. Most of them are raising families. More than twenty have even returned to my high school as teachers. As of this writing, two of my own children have made it through college. I have two more to go. As far as I can tell, most of these young people have "kept the faith" by surviving some of the challenges college life presents to believers. Here are four main challenges to your faith you will likely face when you go away to college, with suggestions for handing them in a positive way:

1. Expect to meet classmates who will disagree with you about everything from music to politics to your attitude to authority to religion. The list is endless. In general, there is a "live-and-let-live" attitude toward all these issues.

   Many of your classmates will have absorbed the morality of popular culture that holds that all values are merely a matter of taste. This conventional morality denies any absolutes in right or wrong. Thus, it contradicts Christ and the church's teachings that some behaviors are wrong despite the circumstances or a person's intention. You may actually hold a minority position on issues like abortion and the value of chastity.

2. You will likely have professors who will ridicule religion, belittle the Catholic church, and deny the divinity of Jesus. Don't let this surprise or shock you. Many of them have also rejected absolute truth. Religion, especially the Catholic faith, which is the largest denomination in the United States, threatens many people.

3. You might encounter some fundamentalist religious groups on campus who will try to win you over to their religion. Their evangelistic outreach can be at times overwhelming. Tell them you are a Catholic. Let them know that you have professed faith in Christ since the time of your baptism. Make sure to connect with a Catholic community on or near campus (see below).

4. The biggest threat to your faith is likely to be yourself! You will be tempted to cave in to the various freedoms of college life. These temptations are especially strong in the areas of sex, drinking, and drugs. But remember, the inappropriateness of these actions does not change because of your new environment or because others are doing them.

One excellent way to "keep the faith" at college is to find like-minded friends, including a roommate, who share your Catholic faith and values. They can help you keep your standards and find good, healthy ways to have fun without going along with what everyone else is doing. These friends can also go to Mass with you, a practice that goes by the wayside with too many college students.

Another help is Catholic campus ministry, a service present on both Catholic and non-Catholic campuses. The purposes of campus ministry include forming faith communities, helping students live the faith by forming Christian consciences, educating for justice, and aiding religious development.

Campus ministry may sponsor organizations like the Newman Club, a longtime Catholic organization on college campuses. Former students of mine have joined organizations like these, often emerging as leaders. They have told me what a lifeline these organization were in helping their Catholic identity grow and develop while in college.

Many campus ministry programs also sponsor Christian life communities, which sometimes share living quarters in a house off campus. You might want to join such a community.

Make sure that when you visit a prospective college, you set up an appointment with the director of Catholic campus ministry. This person will be most happy to tell you about life as a Catholic on that campus.

101

In the last analysis, how will God decide whether or not I get into heaven?

In a word, you must *love*. You must love God above all else, with all your heart, with all your soul, with all your mind, and with all your strength. And you must love your neighbor as yourself (cf. Mk 12:28-34). To expand:

◆ Loving God with all your heart means loving God with all your desires and inclinations. Do you desire God to be first in your life? Or does something else take God's place: pleasure, popularity, possessions, power? If you make something else your God, you are on the wrong path to heaven.

◆ Loving God with all your soul means loving God with your very life. Have you chosen God as the goal of your life? Are you willing to commit your life to God—by serving God and following God's will? Would you be willing to give up your life for God?

◆ Loving God with all of your mind means you keep God in your thoughts. It means you have an active prayer life, talking and listening to the Lord as your best friend. If God would forget you for an instant, you would cease to exist. But how often do you think of God? Do silly, trivial thoughts distract you from what is really important? Do you pray to God often?

◆ Loving God with all your strength means your energy goes into doing God's will, not to accumulating worldly riches and honors. Only what God thinks of you is important. All else is secondary.

How do you love the invisible God you do not see? By loving God's creations—especially the people around you. Begin by loving yourself. First, thank God for creating you and giving you marvelous gifts. Second, love yourself by respecting yourself. Third, develop the gifts God has given you. Fourth, use those gifts for other people.

In the parable of the Last Judgment in Matthew's gospel, Jesus explains that the basis of judgment is simple: Did you feed the hungry, give drink to the thirsty, and welcome the stranger? Did you clothe the naked and visit the sick and imprisoned? In other words, whatever you do—or fail to do—to and for others will come back to you. And this is especially true if you respond to or neglect those least of God's children.

Once again, Jesus will ask you one simple question at judgment time: "Did you love—God, neighbor, self." If you can answer yes, then God will reward you in heaven beyond what you can possibly imagine.

Notes

Chapter 1

1. Adapted from Donald Grey Barnhouse, *Let Me Illustrate* (Grand Rapids, MI: Fleming H. Revell, 1967), p. 231.

Chapter 3

1. Quoted in *Searching for Meaning* (Winona, MN: St. Mary's College Press, 1970), p. 80.

2. Raymond E. Brown, quoted in Michael L. Cook, S.J., *Responses to 101 Questions About Jesus* (New York: Paulist Press, 1993), p. 29. For an excellent discussion of this question about Jesus' self-knowledge, you might enjoy reading Raymond E. Brown, *Responses to 101 Questions on the Bible* (New York: Paulist Press, 1990), pp. 97-99, and Joseph A. Fitzmyer, S.J., *A Christological Catechism: New Testament Answers*, new and revised edition (New York: Paulist Press, 1991), pp. 97-100.

3. Raymond E. Brown, p. 99.

4. George Gallup, Jr., and Jim Castelli, *The People's Religion, American Faith in the 90s* (New York: Macmillan, 1989), p. 58.

5. See John P. Meier, *A Marginal Jew, II* (New York: Doubleday, 1994), p. 528.

6. Kenneth L. Woodward, *Making Saints* (New York: Simon and Schuster, 1990.) This is an excellent book. It discusses not only the process of how the church canonizes saints, but also reviews the lives of some extraordinary Christians like Dorothy Day.

7. Meier, p. 512.

Chapter 5

1. John Deedy, *Retrospect* (Chicago: Thomas More Press, 1990), p. 52.

2. Jull Haak Adels, ed., *The Wisdom of the Saints*, (New York: Oxford University Press, 1987), p. 23.

Chapter 6

1. Basil Pennington, O.C.S.O., *Challenges in Prayer* (Wilmington, DE: Michael Glazier, Inc., 1982), pp. 61-62.

2. Haak Adels, p. 54.

what we really want to know....

St. Bridget's Church
Youth Ministry
6006 Three Chopt Rd.
Richmond, VA 23226

© 1993 Warner